A

DISQUISITION

ON

GOVERNMENT

BY

JOHN C. CALHOUN.

EDITED BY

RICHARD K. CRALLE.

MARTINO FINE BOOKS
Eastford, CT 06242
2016

Martino Fine Books
P.O. Box 913,
Eastford, CT 06242 USA

ISBN 978-1-68422-025-0

© *2016 Martino Fine Books*

Cover Design Tiziana Matarazzo

Printed in the United States of America On 100% Acid-Free Paper

A

DISQUISITION

ON

GOVERNMENT

BY

JOHN C. CALHOUN.

EDITED BY

RICHARD K. CRALLE.

NEW YORK
PETER SMITH
1943

First Published 1853
Reprinted 1943

A DISQUISITION ON GOVERNMENT.

In order to have a clear and just conception of the nature and object of government, it is indispensable to understand correctly what that constitution or law of our nature is, in which government originates; or, to express it more fully and accurately,—that law, without which government would not, and with which, it must necessarily exist. Without this, it is as impossible to lay any solid foundation for the science of government, as it would be to lay one for that of astronomy, without a like understanding of that constitution or law of the material world, according to which the several bodies composing the solar system mutually act on each other, and by which they are kept in their respective spheres. The first question, accordingly, to be considered is,—What is that constitution or law of our nature, without which government would not exist, and with which its existence is necessary?

In considering this, I assume, as an incontestable fact, that man is so constituted as to be a social being. His inclinations and wants, physical and moral, irresistibly impel him to associate with his kind; and he has, accordingly, never been found, in any age or country, in any state other than the social. In no other, indeed, could he exist; and in no other, —were it possible for him to exist,—could he attain to a full development of his moral and intellectual faculties, or raise himself, in the scale of being, much above the level of the brute creation.

I next assume, also, as a fact not less incontestable, that, while man is so constituted as to make the social state necessary to his existence and the full development of his faculties, this state itself cannot exist without government. The assumption rests on universal experience. In no age or country has any society or community ever been found, whether enlightened or savage, without government of some description.

Having assumed these, as unquestionable phenomena of our nature, I shall, without further remark, proceed to the investigation of the primary and important question,—What is that constitution of our nature, which, while it impels man to associate with his kind, renders it impossible for society to exist without government?

The answer will be found in the fact, (not less incontestable than either of the others,) that, while man is created for the social state, and is accordingly so formed as to feel what affects others, as well as what affects himself, he is, at the same time, so constituted as to feel more intensely what affects him directly, than what affects him indirectly through others; or, to express it differently, he is so constituted, that his direct or individual affections are stronger than his sympathetic or social feelings. I intentionally avoid the expression, *selfish* feelings, as applicable to the former; because, as commonly used, it implies an unusual excess of the individual over the social feelings, in the person to whom it is applied; and, consequently, something depraved and vicious. My object is, to exclude such inference, and to restrict the inquiry exclusively to facts in their bearings on the subject under consideration, viewed as mere phenomena appertaining to our nature,—constituted as it is; and which are as unquestionable as is that of gravitation, or any other phenomenon of the material world.

In asserting that our individual are stronger than our social feelings, it is not intended to deny that there are instances, growing out of peculiar relations,—as that of a mother and her infant,—or resulting from the force of education and habit over peculiar constitutions, in which the latter have overpowered the former; but these instances are few, and always regarded as something extraordinary. The deep impression they make, whenever they occur, is the strongest proof that they are regarded as exceptions to some general and well understood law of our nature; just as some of the minor powers of the material world are apparently to gravitation.

I might go farther, and assert this to be a phenomenon, not of our nature only, but of all animated existence, throughout its entire range, so far as our knowledge extends. It would, indeed, seem to be essentially connected with the great law of self-preservation which pervades all that feels, from man down to the lowest and most insignificant reptile or insect. In none is it stronger than in man. His social feelings may, indeed, in a state of safety and abundance, combined with high intellectual and moral culture, acquire great expansion and force; but not so great as to overpower this all-pervading and essential law of animated existence.

But that constitution of our nature which makes us feel more intensely what affects us directly than what affects us indirectly through others, necessarily leads to conflict between individuals. Each, in consequence, has a greater regard for his own safety or happiness, than for the safety or happiness of others; and, where these come in opposition, is ready to sacrifice the interests of others to his own. And hence, the tendency to a universal state of conflict, between individual and individual; accompanied by the connected passions of suspicion, jealousy, anger and revenge,—followed by insolence, fraud and cruelty;—and, if not prevented by some controlling power, ending in a state of universal discord and confusion, destructive of the social state and the ends for which it is ordained. This controlling power, wherever vested, or by whomsoever exercised, is GOVERNMENT.

It follows, then, that man is so constituted, that government is necessary to the existence of society, and society to his existence, and the perfection of his faculties. It follows, also, that government has its origin in this twofold constitution of his nature ; the sympathetic or social feelings constituting the remote, —and the individual or direct, the proximate cause.

If man had been differently constituted in either particular ;—if, instead of being social in his nature, he had been created without sympathy for his kind, and independent of others for his safety and existence; or if, on the other hand, he had been so created, as to feel more intensely what affected others than what affected himself, (if that were possible,) or, even, had this supposed interest been equal,— it is manifest that, in either case, there would have been no necessity for government, and that none would ever have existed. But, although society and government are thus intimately connected with and dependent on each other,—of the two society is the greater. It is the first in the order of things, and in the dignity of its object; that of society being primary,—to preserve and perfect our race; and that of government secondary and subordinate, to preserve and perfect society. Both are, however, necessary to the existence and well-being of our race, and equally of Divine ordination.

I have said,—if it were possible for man to be so constituted, as to feel what affects others more strongly than what affects himself, or even as strongly,—because, it may be well doubted, whether the stronger feeling or affection of individuals for themselves, combined with a feebler and subordinate feeling or affection for others, is not, in beings of limited reason and faculties, a constitution necessary to their preservation and existence. If reversed,—if their feelings and affections were stronger for others than for themselves, or even as strong, the necessary result would seem to be, that all individuality would be lost; and boundless and remediless disorder and confusion would ensue. For each, at the same moment, intensely participating in all the conflicting emotions of those around him, would, of course, forget himself and all that concerned him immediately, in his officious intermeddling with the affairs of all others; which, from his limited reason and faculties, he could neither properly understand nor manage. Such a state of things would, as far as we can see, lead to endless disorder and confusion, not less destructive to our race than a state of anarchy. It would, besides, be remediless,—for government would be impossible; or, if it could by possibility exist, its object would be reversed. Selfishness would have to be encouraged, and benevolence discouraged. Individuals would have to be encouraged, by rewards, to become more selfish, and deterred, by punishments, from being too benevolent; and this, too, by a government, administered by those who, on the supposition, would have the greatest aversion for selfishness and the highest admiration for benevolence.

To the Infinite Being, the Creator of all, belongs exclusively the care and superintendence of the whole. He, in his infinite wisdom and goodness, has allotted to every class of animated beings its condition and appropriate functions; and has endowed each with feelings, instincts, capacities, and faculties, best adapted to its allotted condition. To man, he has assigned the social and political state, as best adapted to develop the great capacities and faculties, intellectual and moral, with which he has endowed him; and has, accordingly, constituted him so as not only to impel him into the social state, but to make government necessary for his preservation and well-being.

But government, although intended to protect and preserve society, has itself a strong tendency to disorder and abuse of its powers, as all experience and almost every page of history testify. The cause is to be found in the same constitution of our nature which makes government indispensable. The powers which it is necessary for government to possess, in order to repress violence and preserve order, cannot execute themselves. They must be administered by men in whom, like others, the individual are stronger than the social feelings. And hence, the powers vested in them to prevent injustice and oppression on the part of others, will, if left unguarded, be by them converted into instruments to oppress the rest of the community. That, by which this is prevented, by whatever name called, is what is meant by CONSTITUTION, in its most comprehensive sense, when applied to GOVERNMENT.

Having its origin in the same principle of our nature, *constitution* stands to *government*, as *government* stands to *society;* and, as the end for which society is ordained, would be defeated without government, so that for which government is ordained would, in a great measure, be defeated without constitution. But they differ in this striking particular. There is no difficulty in forming government. It is not even a matter of choice, whether there shall be one or not. Like breathing, it is not permitted to depend on our volition. Necessity will force it on all communities in some one form or another. Very different is the case as to constitution. Instead of a matter of necessity, it is one of the most difficult tasks imposed on man to form a constitution worthy of the name; while, to form a perfect one,—one that would completely counteract the tendency of government to oppression and abuse, and hold it strictly to the great ends for which it is ordained,—has thus far exceeded human wisdom, and possibly ever will. From this, another striking difference results. Constitution is the contrivance of man, while government is of Divine ordination. Man is left to perfect what the wisdom of the Infinite ordained, as necessary to preserve the race.

With these remarks, I proceed to the consideration of the important and difficult question: How is this tendency of government to be counteracted? Or, to express it more fully,—How can those who are invested with the powers of government be prevented from employing them, as the means of aggrandizing themselves, instead of using them to protect and preserve society? It cannot be done by instituting a higher power to control the government, and those who administer it. This would be but to change the seat of authority, and to make this higher power, in reality, the government; with the same tendency, on the part of those who might control its powers, to pervert them into instruments of aggrandizement. Nor can it be done by limiting the powers of government, so as to make it too feeble to be made an instrument of abuse; for, passing by the difficulty of so limiting its powers, without creating a power higher than the government itself to enforce the observance of the limitations, it is a sufficient objection that it would, if practicable, defeat the end for which government is ordained, by making it too feeble to protect and preserve society. The powers necessary for this purpose will ever prove sufficient to aggrandize those who control it, at the expense of the rest of the community.

In estimating what amount of power would be requisite to secure the objects of government, we must take into the reckoning, what would be necessary to defend the community against external, as well as internal dangers. Government must be able to repel assaults from abroad, as well as to repress violence and disorders within. It must not be overlooked, that the human race is not comprehended in a single society or community. The limited reason and faculties of man, the great diversity of language, customs, pursuits, situation and complexion, and the difficulty of intercourse, with various other causes, have, by their operation, formed a great many separate communities, acting independently of each other. Between these there is the same tendency to conflict,—and from the same constitution of our nature,—as between men individually; and even stronger,—because the sympathetic or social feelings are not so strong between different communities, as between individuals of the same community. So powerful, indeed, is this tendency, that it has led to almost incessant wars between contiguous communities for plunder and conquest, or to avenge injuries, real or supposed.

So long as this state of things continues, exigencies will occur, in which the entire powers and resources of the community will be needed to defend its existence. When this is at stake, every other consideration must yield to it. Self-preservation is the supreme law, as well with communities as individuals. And hence the danger of withholding from government the full command of the power and resources of the state; and the great difficulty of limiting its powers consistently with the protection and preservation of the community. And hence the question recurs,—By what means can government, without being divested of the full command of the resources of the community, be prevented from abusing its powers?

The question involves difficulties which, from the earliest ages, wise and good men have attempted to overcome;—but hitherto with but partial success. For this purpose many devices have been resorted to, suited to the various stages of intelligence and civilization through which our race has passed, and to the different forms of government to which they have been applied. The aid of superstition, ceremonies, education, religion, organic arrangements, both of the government and the community, has been, from time to time, appealed to. Some of the most remarkable of these devices, whether regarded in reference to their wisdom and the skill displayed in their application, or to the permanency of their effects, are to be found in the early dawn of civilization ;—in the institutions of the Egyptians, the Hindoos, the Chinese, and the Jews. The only materials which that early age afforded for the construction of constitutions, when intelligence was so partially diffused, were applied with consummate wisdom and skill. To their successful application may be fairly traced the subsequent advance of our race in civilization and intelligence, of which we now enjoy the benefits. For, without a constitution,—something to counteract the strong tendency of government to disorder and abuse, and to give stability to political institutions,—there can be little progress or permanent improvement.

In answering the important question under consideration, it is not necessary to enter into an examination of the various contrivances adopted by these celebrated governments to counteract this tendency to disorder and abuse, nor to undertake to treat of constitution in its most comprehensive sense. What I propose is far more limited,—to explain on what principles government must be formed, in order to resist, by its own interior structure,—or, to use a single term, *organism*,—the tendency to abuse of power. This structure, or organism, is what is meant by constitution, in its strict and more usual sense; and it is this which distinguishes, what are called, constitutional governments from absolute. It is in this strict and more usual sense that I propose to use the term hereafter.

How government, then, must be constructed, in order to counteract, through its organism, this tendency on the part of those who make and execute the laws to oppress those subject to their operation, is the next question which claims attention.

There is but one way in which this can possibly be done ; and that is, by such an organism as will furnish the ruled with the means of resisting successfully this tendency on the part of the rulers to oppression and abuse. Power can only be resisted by power,—and tendency by tendency. Those who exercise power and those subject to its exercise,—the rulers and the ruled,—stand in antagonistic relations to each other. The same constitution of our nature which leads rulers to oppress the ruled,—regardless of the object for which government is ordained,—will, with equal strength, lead the ruled to resist, when possessed of the means of making peaceable and effective resistance. Such an organism, then, as will furnish the means by which resistance may be systematically and peaceably made on the part of the ruled, to oppression and abuse of power on the part of the rulers, is the first and indispensable step towards *forming* a constitutional government. And as this can only be effected by or through the right of suffrage,—(the right on the part of the ruled to choose their rulers at proper intervals, and to hold them thereby responsible for their conduct,)—the responsibility of the rulers to the ruled, through the right of suffrage, is the indispensable and primary principle in the *foundation* of a constitutional government. When this right is properly guarded, and the people sufficiently enlightened to understand their own rights and the interests of the community, and duly to appreciate the motives and conduct of those appointed to make and execute the laws, it is all-sufficient to give to those who elect, effective control over those they have elected.

I call the right of suffrage the indispensable and primary principle; for it would be a great and dangerous mistake to suppose, as many do, that it is, of itself, sufficient to form constitutional governments. To this erroneous opinion may be traced one of the causes, why so few attempts to form constitutional governments have succeeded; and why, of the few which have, so small a number have had durable existence. It has led, not only to mistakes in the attempts to form such governments, but to their overthrow, when they have, by some good fortune, been correctly formed. So far from being, of itself, sufficient,—however well guarded it might be, and however enlightened the people,—it would, unaided by other provisions, leave the government as absolute, as it would be in the hands of irresponsible rulers; and with a tendency, at least as strong, towards oppression and abuse of its powers; as I shall next proceed to explain.

The right of suffrage, of itself, can do no more than give complete control to those who elect, over the conduct of those they have elected. In doing this, it accomplishes all it possibly can accomplish. This is its aim,—and when this is attained, its end is fulfilled. It can do no more, however enlightened the people, or however widely extended or well guarded the right may be. The sum total, then, of its effects, when most successful, is, to make those elected, the true and faithful representatives of those who elected them,—instead of irresponsible rulers, —as they would be without it; and thus, by converting it into an agency, and the rulers into agents, to divest government of all claims to sovereignty, and to retain it unimpaired to the community. But it is manifest that the right of suffrage, in making these changes, transfers, in reality, the actual control over the government, from those who make and execute the laws, to the body of the community; and, thereby, places the powers of the government as fully in the mass of the community, as they would be if they, in fact, had assembled, made, and executed the laws themselves, without the intervention of representatives or agents. The more perfectly it does this, the more perfectly it accomplishes its ends; but in doing so, it only changes the seat of authority, without counteracting, in the least, the tendency of the government to oppression and abuse of its powers.

If the whole community had the same interests, so that the interests of each and every portion would be so affected by the action of the government, that the laws which oppressed or impoverished one portion, would necessarily oppress and impoverish all others,—or the reverse,—then the right of suffrage, of itself, would be all-sufficient to counteract the tendency of the government to oppression and abuse of its powers; and, of course, would form, of itself, a perfect constitutional government. The interest of all being the same, by supposition, as far as the action of the government was concerned, all would have like interests as to what laws should be made, and how they should be executed. All strife and struggle would cease as to who should be elected to make and execute them. The only question would be, who was most fit; who the wisest and most capable of understanding the common interest of the whole. This decided, the election would pass off quietly, and without party discord; as no one portion could advance its own peculiar interest without regard to the rest, by electing a favorite candidate.

But such is not the case. On the contrary, nothing is more difficult than to equalize the action of the government, in reference to the various and diversified interests of the community; and nothing more easy than to pervert its powers into instruments to aggrandize and enrich one or more interests by oppressing and impoverishing the others; and this too, under the operation of laws, couched in general terms;—and which, on their face, appear fair and equal. Nor is this the case in some particular communities only. It is so in all; the small and the great,—the poor and the rich,—irrespective of pursuits, productions, or degrees of civilization; —with, however, this difference, that the more extensive and populous the country, the more diversified the condition and pursuits of its population, and the richer, more luxurious, and dissimilar the people, the more difficult is it to equalize the action of the government,—and the more easy for one portion of the community to pervert its powers to oppress, and plunder the other.

Such being the case, it necessarily results, that the right of suffrage, by placing the control of the government in the community must, from the same constitution of our nature which makes government necessary to preserve society, lead to conflict among its different interests,—each striving to obtain possession of its powers, as the means of protecting itself against the others;—or of advancing its respective interests, regardless of the interests of others. For this purpose, a struggle will take place between the various interests to obtain a majority, in order to control the government. If no one interest be strong enough, of itself, to obtain it, a combination will be formed between those whose interests are most alike;—each conceding something to the others, until a sufficient number is obtained to make a majority. The process may be slow, and much time may be required before a compact, organized majority can be thus formed; but formed it will be in time, even without preconcert or design, by the sure workings of that principle or constitution of our nature in which government itself originates. When once formed, the community will be divided into two great parties,—a major and minor,—between which there will be incessant struggles on the one side to retain, and on the other to obtain the majority,—and, thereby, the control of the government and the advantages it confers.

So deeply seated, indeed, is this tendency to conflict between the different interests or portions of the community, that it would result from the action of the government itself, even though it were possible to find a community, where the people were all of the same pursuits, placed in the same condition of life, and in every respect, so situated, as to be without inequality of condition or diversity of interests. The advantages of possessing the control of the powers of the government, and, thereby, of its honors and emoluments, are, of themselves, exclusive of all other considerations, ample to divide even such a community into two great hostile parties.

In order to form a just estimate of the full force of these advantages,—without reference to any other consideration,—it must be remembered, that government,—to fulfill the ends for which it is ordained, and more especially that of protection against external dangers,—must, in the present condition of the world, be clothed with powers sufficient to call forth the resources of the community, and be prepared, at all times, to command them promptly in every emergency which may possibly arise. For this purpose large establishments are necessary, both civil and military, (including naval, where, from situation, that description of force may be required,) with all the means necessary for prompt and effective action,—such as fortifications, fleets, armories, arsenals, magazines, arms of all descriptions, with well-trained forces, in sufficient numbers to wield them with skill and energy,

whenever the occasion requires it. The administration and management of a government with such
vast establishments must necessarily require a host
of employees, agents, and officers;—of whom many
must be vested with high and responsible trusts,
and occupy exalted stations, accompanied with much
influence and patronage. To meet the necessary
expenses, large sums must be collected and dis-
bursed; and, for this purpose, heavy taxes must be
imposed, requiring a multitude of officers for their
collection and disbursement. The whole united
must necessarily place under the control of government an amount of honors and emoluments, sufficient to excite profoundly the ambition of the aspiring and the cupidity of the avaricious; and to lead
to the formation of hostile parties, and violent party conflicts and struggles to obtain the control of
the government. And what makes this evil remediless, through the right of suffrage of itself, however
modified or carefully guarded, or however enlightened the people, is the fact that, as far as the honors
and emoluments of the government and its fiscal
action are concerned, it is impossible to equalize it.
The reason is obvious. Its honors and emoluments,
however great, can fall to the lot of but a few, compared to the entire number of the community, and
the multitude who will seek to participate in them.
But, without this, there is a reason which renders it
impossible to equalize the action of the government,
so far as its fiscal operation extends,—which I shall
next explain.

Few, comparatively, as they are, the agents and

employees of the government constitute that portion of the community who are the exclusive recipients of the proceeds of the taxes. Whatever amount is taken from the community, in the form of taxes, if not lost, goes to them in the shape of expenditures or disbursements. The two,—disbursement and taxation,—constitute the fiscal action of the government. They are correlatives. What the one takes from the community, under the name of taxes, is transferred to the portion of the community who are the recipients, under that of disbursements. But, as the recipients constitute only a portion of the community, it follows, taking the two parts of the fiscal process together, that its action must be unequal between the payers of the taxes and the recipients of their proceeds. Nor can it be otherwise, unless what is collected from each individual in the shape of taxes, shall be returned to him, in that of disbursements; which would make the process nugatory and absurd. Taxation may, indeed, be made equal, regarded separately from disbursement. Even this is no easy task; but the two united cannot possibly be made equal.

Such being the case, it must necessarily follow, that some one portion of the community must pay in taxes more than it receives back in disbursements; while another receives in disbursements more than it pays in taxes. It is, then, manifest, taking the whole process together, that taxes must be, in effect, bounties to that portion of the community which receives more in disbursements than it pays in taxes; while, to the other which pays in taxes more than it receives in disbursements, they are taxes in reality,—burthens, instead of bounties. This consequence is unavoidable. It results from the nature of the process, be the taxes ever so equally laid, and the disbursements ever so fairly made, in reference to the public service.

It is assumed, in coming to this conclusion, that the disbursements are made within the community. The reasons assigned would not be applicable if the proceeds of the taxes were paid in tribute, or expended in foreign countries. In either of these cases, the burthen would fall on all, in proportion to the amount of taxes they respectively paid.

Nor would it be less a bounty to the portion of the community which received back in disbursements more than it paid in taxes, because received as salaries for official services; or payments to persons employed in executing the works required by the government; or furnishing it with its various supplies; or any other description of public employment,—instead of being bestowed gratuitously. It is the disbursements which give additional, and, usually, very profitable and honorable employments to the portion of the community where they are made. But to create such employments, by disbursements, is to bestow on the portion of the community to whose lot the disbursements may fall, a far more durable and lasting benefit,—one that would add much more to its wealth and population,—than would the bestowal of an equal sum gratuitously : and hence, to the extent that the disbursements exceed the taxes, it may be fairly regarded as a bounty.

The very reverse is the case in reference to the portion which pays in taxes more than it receives in disbursements. With them, profitable employments are diminished to the same extent, and population and wealth correspondingly decreased.

The necessary result, then, of the unequal fiscal action of the government is, to divide the community into two great classes; one consisting of those who, in reality, pay the taxes, and, of course, bear exclusively the burthen of supporting the government; and the other, of those who are the recipients of their proceeds, through disbursements, and who are, in fact, supported by the government; or, in fewer words, to divide it into tax-payers and tax-consumers.

But the effect of this is to place them in antagonistic relations, in reference to the fiscal action of the government, and the entire course of policy therewith connected. For, the greater the taxes and disbursements, the greater the gain of the one and the loss of the other,—and *vice versa;* and consequently, the more the policy of the government is calculated to increase taxes and disbursements, the more it will be favored by the one and opposed by the other.

The effect, then, of every increase is, to enrich and strengthen the one, and impoverish and weaken the other. This, indeed, may be carried to such an extent, that one class or portion of the community may be elevated to wealth and power, and the other depressed to abject poverty and dependence, simply by the fiscal action of the government; and this too, through disbursements only,—even under a system of equal taxes imposed for revenue only. If such may be the effect of taxes and disbursements, when confined to their legitimate objects,—that of raising revenue for the public service,—some conception may be formed, how one portion of the community may be crushed, and another elevated on its ruins, by systematically perverting the power of taxation and disbursement, for the purpose of aggrandizing and building up one portion of the community at the expense of the other. That it *will* be so used, unless prevented, is, from the constitution of man, just as certain as that it *can* be so used; and that, if not prevented, it must give rise to two parties, and to violent conflicts and struggles between them, to obtain the control of the government, is, for the same reason, not less certain.

Nor is it less certain, from the operation of all these causes, that the dominant majority, for the time, would have the same tendency to oppression and abuse of power, which, without the right of suffrage, irresponsible rulers would have. No reason, indeed, can be assigned, why the latter would abuse their power, which would not apply, with equal force, to the former. The dominant majority, for the time, would, in reality, through the right of suffrage, be the rulers—the controlling, governing, and irresponsible power; and those who make and execute the laws would, for the time, be, in reality, but *their* representatives and agents.

Nor would the fact that the former would constitute a majority of the community, counteract a tendency originating in the constitution of man; and which, as such, cannot depend on the number by whom the powers of the government may be wielded. Be it greater or smaller, a majority or minority, it must equally partake of an attribute inherent in each individual composing it; and, as in each the individual is stronger than the social feelings, the one would have the same tendency as the other to oppression and abuse of power. The reason applies to government in all its forms,— whether it be that of the one, the few, or the many. In each there must, of necessity, be a governing and governed,—a ruling and a subject portion. The one implies the other; and in all, the two bear the same relation to each other;—and have, on the part of the governing portion, the same tendency to oppression and abuse of power. Where the majority is that portion, it matters not how its powers may be exercised;—whether directly by themselves, or indirectly, through representatives or agents. Be it which it may, the minority, for the time, will be as much the governed or subject portion, as are the people in an aristocracy, or the subjects in a monarchy. The only difference in this respect is, that in the government of a majority, the minority may become the majority, and the majority the minority, through the right of suffrage; and thereby change their relative positions, without the intervention of force and revolution. But the duration, or uncertainty of the tenure, by which power is held, cannot, of itself, counteract the tendency inherent in government to oppression and abuse of power. On the contrary, the very uncertainty of the tenure, combined with the violent party warfare which must ever precede a change of parties under such governments, would rather tend to increase than diminish the tendency to oppression.

As, then, the right of suffrage, without some other provision, cannot counteract this tendency of government, the next question for consideration is —What is that other provision? This demands the most serious consideration; for of all the questions embraced in the science of government, it involves a principle, the most important, and the least understood; and when understood, the most difficult of application in practice. It is, indeed, emphatically, that principle which *makes* the constitution, in its strict and limited sense.

From what has been said, it is manifest, that this provision must be of a character calculated to prevent any one interest, or combination of interests, from using the powers of government to aggrandize itself at the expense of the others. Here lies the evil: and just in proportion as it shall prevent, or fail to prevent it, in the same degree it will effect, or fail to effect the end intended to be accomplished. There is but one certain mode in which this result can be secured; and that is, by the adoption of some restriction or limitation, which shall so effectually prevent any one interest, or combination of interests, from obtaining the exclusive control of the government, as to render hopeless all attempts directed to that end. There is, again, but one mode in which this can be effected; and that is, by taking the sense of each interest or portion of the community, which may be unequally and injuriously affected by the action of the government, separately, through its own majority, or in some other way by which its voice may be fairly expressed; and to require the consent of each interest, either to put or to keep the government in action. This, too, can be accomplished only in one way,—and that is, by such an organism of the government,—and, if necessary for the purpose, of the community also,—as will, by dividing and distributing the powers of government, give to each division or interest, through its appropriate organ, either a concurrent voice in making and executing the laws, or a veto on their execution. It is only by such an organism, that the assent of each can be made necessary to put the government in motion; or the power made effectual to arrest its action, when put in motion;—and it is only by the one or the other that the different interests, orders, classes, or portions, into which the community may be divided, can be protected, and all conflict and struggle between them prevented,— by rendering it impossible to put or to keep it in action, without the concurrent consent of all.

Such an organism as this, combined with the right of suffrage, constitutes, in fact, the elements of constitutional government. The one, by rendering those who make and execute the laws responsible to those on whom they operate, prevents the rulers from oppressing the ruled; and the other, by making it impossible for any one interest or

combination of interests or class, or order, or portion of the community, to obtain exclusive control,
prevents any one of them from oppressing the
other. It is clear, that oppression and abuse of
power must come, if at all, from the one or the other
quarter. From no other can they come. It follows,
that the two, suffrage and proper organism combined, are sufficient to counteract the tendency of
government to oppression and abuse of power; and
to restrict it to the fulfilment of the great ends for
which it is ordained.

In coming to this conclusion, I have assumed the
organism to be perfect, and the different interests,
portions, or classes of the community, to be sufficiently enlightened to understand its character and
object, and to exercise, with due intelligence, the
right of suffrage. To the extent that either may
be defective, to the same extent the government
would fall short of fulfilling its end. But this does
not impeach the truth of the principles on which it
rests. In reducing them to proper form, in apply-
ing them to practical uses, all elementary principles are liable to difficulties; but they are not, on
this account, the less true, or valuable. Where the
organism is perfect, every interest will be truly and
fully represented, and of course the whole community must be so. It may be difficult, or even impossible, to make a perfect organism,—but, although
this be true, yet even when, instead of the sense
of each and of all, it takes that of a few great and
prominent interests only, it would still, in a great
measure, if not altogether, fulfil the end intended

by a constitution. For, in such case, it would require so large a portion of the community, compared
with the whole, to concur, or acquiesce in the action
of the government, that the number to be plundered would be too few, and the number to be aggran-
dized too many, to afford adequate motives to oppression and the abuse of its powers. Indeed, however imperfect the organism, it must have more or
less effect in diminishing such tendency.

It may be readily inferred, from what has been
stated, that the effect of organism is neither to supersede nor diminish the importance of the right
of suffrage ; but to aid and perfect it. The object
of the latter is, to collect the sense of the community. The more fully and perfectly it accomplishes
this, the more fully and perfectly it fulfils its end.
But the most it can do, of itself, is to collect the
sense of the greater number ; that is, of the stronger
interests, or combination of interests ; and to assume
this to be the sense of the community. It is only
when aided by a proper organism, that it can collect the sense of the entire community,—of each and
all its interests ; of each, through its appropriate
organ, and of the whole, through all of them united.
This would truly be the sense of the entire community ; for whatever diversity each interest might
have within itself,—-as all would have the same interest in reference to the action of the government,
the individuals composing each would be fully and
truly represented by its own majority or appropriate
organ, regarded in reference to the other interests.
In brief, every individual of every interest might

trust, with confidence, its majority or appropriate organ, against that of every other interest.

It results, from what has been said, that there are two different modes in which the sense of the community may be taken; one, simply by the right of suffrage, unaided; the other, by the right through a proper organism. Each collects the sense of the majority. But one regards numbers only, and considers the whole community as a unit, having but one common interest throughout; and collects the sense of the greater number of the whole, as that of the community. The other, on the contrary, regards interests as well as numbers;—considering the community as made up of different and conflicting interests, as far as the action of the government is concerned; and takes the sense of each, through its majority or appropriate organ, and the united sense of all, as the sense of the entire community. The former of these I shall call the numerical, or absolute majority; and the latter, the concurrent, or constitutional majority. I call it the constitutional majority, because it is an essential element in every constitutional government,—be its form what it may. So great is the difference, politically speaking, between the two majorities, that they cannot be confounded, without leading to great and fatal errors; and yet the distinction between them has been so entirely overlooked, that when the term *majority* is used in political discussions, it is applied exclusively to designate the numerical,—as if there were no other. Until this distinction is recognized, and better understood, there will continue to be great liability to error in properly constructing constitutional governments, especially of the popular form, and of preserving them when properly constructed. Until then, the latter will have a strong tendency to slide, first, into the government of the numerical majority, and, finally, into absolute government of some other form. To show that such must be the case, and at the same time to mark more strongly the difference between the two, in order to guard against the danger of overlooking it, I propose to consider the subject more at length.

The first and leading error which naturally arises from overlooking the distinction referred to, is, to confound the numerical majority with the people; and this so completely as to regard them as identical. This is a consequence that necessarily results from considering the numerical as the only majority. All admit, that a popular government, or democracy, is the government of the people; for the terms imply this. A perfect government of the kind would be one which would embrace the consent of every citizen or member of the community; but as this is impracticable, in the opinion of those who regard the numerical as the only majority, and who can perceive no other way by which the sense of the people can be taken,—they are compelled to adopt this as the only true basis of popular government, in contradistinction to governments of the aristocratical or monarchical form. Being thus constrained, they are, in the next place, forced to regard the numerical majority, as, in effect, the entire people; that is, the greater part as the whole; and the government of the greater part as the government of the whole. It is thus the two come to be confounded, and a part made identical with the whole. And it is thus, also, that all the rights, powers, and immunities of the whole people come to be attributed to the numerical majority; and, among others, the supreme, sovereign authority of establishing and abolishing governments at pleasure.

This radical error, the consequence of confounding the two, and of regarding the numerical as the only majority, has contributed more than any other cause, to prevent the formation of popular constitutional governments,—and to destroy them even when they have been formed. It leads to the conclusion that, in their formation and establishment, nothing more is necessary than the right of suffrage,—and the allotment to each division of the community a representation in the government, in proportion to numbers. If the numerical majority were really the people; and if, to take its sense truly, were to take the sense of the people truly, a government so constituted would be a true and perfect model of a popular constitutional government; and every departure from it would detract from its excellence. But, as such is not the case,—as the numerical majority, instead of being the people, is only a portion of them,—such a government, instead of being a true and perfect model of the people's government, that is, a people self-governed, is but the government of a part, over a part,—the major over the minor portion.

But this misconception of the true elements of

constitutional government does not stop here. It leads to others equally false and fatal, in reference to the best means of preserving and perpetuating them, when, from some fortunate combination of circumstances, they are correctly formed. For they who fall into these errors regard the restrictions which organism imposes on the will of the numerical majority as restrictions on the will of the people, and, therefore, as not only useless, but wrongful and mischievous. And hence they endeavor to destroy organism, under the delusive hope of making government more democratic.

Such are some of the consequences of confounding the two, and of regarding the numerical as the only majority. And in this may be found the reason why so few popular governments have been properly constructed, and why, of these few, so small a number have proved durable. Such must continue to be the result, so long as these errors continue to be prevalent.

There is another error, of a kindred character, whose influence contributes much to the same results: I refer to the prevalent opinion, that a written constitution, containing suitable restrictions on the powers of government, is sufficient, of itself, without the aid of any organism,—except such as is necessary to separate its several departments, and render them independent of each other,—to counteract the tendency of the numerical majority to oppression and the abuse of power.

A written constitution certainly has many and considerable advantages; but it is a great mistake to suppose, that the mere insertion of provisions to restrict and limit the powers of the government, without investing those for whose protection they are inserted with the means of enforcing their observance, will be sufficient to prevent the major and dominant party from abusing its powers. Being the party in possession of the government, they will, from the same constitution of man which makes government necessary to protect society, be in favor of the powers granted by the constitution, and opposed to the restrictions intended to limit them. As the major and dominant party, they will have no need of these restrictions for their protection. The ballot-box, of itself, would be ample protection to them. Needing no other, they would come, in time, to regard these limitations as unnecessary and improper restraints ;—and endeavor to elude them, with the view of increasing their power and influence.

The minor, or weaker party, on the contrary, would take the opposite direction ;—and regard them as essential to their protection against the dominant party. And, hence, they would endeavor to defend and enlarge the restrictions, and to limit and contract the powers. But where there are no means by which they could compel the major party to observe the restrictions, the only resort left them would be, a strict construction of the constitution, —that is, a construction which would confine these powers to the narrowest limits which the meaning of the words used in the grant would admit.

To this the major party would oppose a liberal

construction,—one which would give to the words of
the grant the broadest meaning of which they were
susceptible.   It would then be construction against
construction; the one to contract, and the other to
enlarge the powers of the government to the utmost.   But of what possible avail could the strict
construction of the minor party be, against the
liberal interpretation of the major, when the one
would have all the powers of the government to
carry its construction into effect,—and the other be
deprived of all means of enforcing its construction?
In a contest so unequal, the result would not be
doubtful. The party in favor of the restrictions would
be overpowered.   At first, they might command
some respect, and do something to stay the march
of encroachment; but they would, in the progress
of the contest, be regarded as mere abstractionists;
and, indeed, deservedly, if they should indulge the
folly of supposing that the party in possession of
the ballot-box and the physical force of the country, could be successfully resisted by an appeal to
reason, truth, justice, or the obligations imposed by
the constitution. For when these, of themselves, shall
exert sufficient influence to stay the hand of power,
then government will be no longer necessary to protect society, nor constitutions needed to prevent
government from abusing its powers.   The end of
the contest would be the subversion of the constitution, either by the undermining process of construction,—where its meaning would admit of possible doubt,—or by substituting in practice what
is called party-usage, in place of its provisions;—

or, finally, when no other contrivance would sub-
serve the purpose, by openly and boldly setting
them aside.   By the one or the other, the restrictions would ultimately be annulled, and the government   be converted into one of unlimited
powers.

Nor would the division of government into separate, and, as it regards each other, independent
departments, prevent this result. Such a division
may do much to facilitate its operations, and to
secure to its administration greater caution and de-
liberation ; but as each and all the departments,—
and, of course, the entire government,—would be
under the control of the numerical majority; it is
too clear to require explanation, that a mere distri-
bution of its powers among its agents or representatives, could do little or nothing to counteract its
tendency to oppression and abuse of power. To
effect this, it would be necessary to go one step
further, and make the several departments the organs of the distinct interests or portions of the community; and to clothe each with a negative on the
others.   But the effect of this would be to change
the government from the numerical into the concurrent majority.

Having now explained the reasons why it is so
difficult to form and preserve popular constitutional
government, so long as the distinction between the
two majorities is overlooked, and the opinion pre-
vails that a written constitution, with suitable restrictions and a proper division of its powers, is sufficient to counteract the tendency of the numerical

majority to the abuse of its power,—I shall next proceed to explain, more fully, why the concurrent majority is an indispensable element in forming constitutional governments; and why the numerical majority, of itself, must, in all cases, make governments absolute.

The necessary consequence of taking the sense of the community by the concurrent majority is, as has been explained, to give to each interest or portion of the community a negative on the others. It is this mutual negative among its various conflicting interests, which invests each with the power of protecting itself;—and places the rights and safety of each, where only they can be securely placed, under its own guardianship. Without this there can be no systematic, peaceful, or effective resistance to the natural tendency of each to come into conflict with the others: and without this there can be no constitution. It is this negative power,—the power of preventing or arresting the action of the government,—be it called by what term it may,—veto, interposition, nullification, check, or balance of power, —which, in fact, forms the constitution. They are all but different names for the negative power. In all its forms, and under all its names, it results from the concurrent majority. Without this there can be no negative; and, without a negative, no constitution. The assertion is true in reference to all constitutional governments, be their forms what they may. It is, indeed, the negative power which makes the constitution,—and the positive which makes the government. The one is the power of acting;—and the other the power of preventing or arresting action. The two, combined, make constitutional governments.

But, as there can be no constitution without the negative power, and no negative power without the concurrent majority;—it follows, necessarily, that where the numerical majority has the sole control of the government, there can be no constitution; as constitution implies limitation or restriction,—and, of course, is inconsistent with the idea of sole or exclusive power. And hence, the numerical, unmixed with the concurrent majority, necessarily forms, in all cases, absolute government.

It is, indeed, the single, or *one power*, which excludes the negative, and constitutes absolute government; and not the *number* in whom the power is vested. The numerical majority is as truly a *single power*, and excludes the negative as completely as the absolute government of one, or of the few. The former is as much the absolute government of the democratic, or popular form, as the latter of the monarchical or aristocratical. It has, accordingly, in common with them, the same tendency to oppression and abuse of power.

Constitutional governments, of whatever form, are, indeed, much more similar to each other, in their structure and character, than they are, respectively, to the absolute governments, even of their own class. All constitutional governments, of whatever class they may be, take the sense of the community by its parts,—each through its appropriate organ; and regard the sense of all its parts, as the sense of the whole. They all rest on the right of suffrage, and the responsibility of rulers, directly or indirectly. On the contrary, all absolute governments, of whatever form, concentrate power in one uncontrolled and irresponsible individual or body, whose will is regarded as the sense of the community. And, hence, the great and broad distinction between governments is,—not that of the one, the few, or the many,—but of the constitutional and the absolute.

From this there results another distinction, which, although secondary in its character, very strongly marks the difference between these forms of government. I refer to their respective conservative principle ;—that is, the principle by which they are upheld and preserved. This principle, in constitutional governments, is *compromise ;*—and in absolute governments, is *force ;*—as will be next explained.

It has been already shown, that the same constitution of man which leads those who govern to oppress the governed,—if not prevented,—will, with equal force and certainty, lead the latter to resist oppression, when possessed of the means of doing so peaceably and successfully. But absolute governments, of all forms, exclude all other means of resistance to their authority, than that of force ; and, of course, leave no other alternative to the governed, but to acquiesce in oppression, however great it may be, or to resort to force to put down the government. But the dread of such a resort must necessarily lead the government to prepare to meet force in order to protect itself; and hence, of necessity, force becomes the conservative principle of all such governments.

On the contrary, the government of the concurrent majority, where the organism is perfect, excludes the possibility of oppression, by giving to each interest, or portion, or order,—where there are established classes,—the means of protecting itself, by its negative, against all measures calculated to advance the peculiar interests of others at its expense. Its effect, then, is, to cause the different interests, portions, or orders,—as the case may be,—to desist from attempting to adopt any measure calculated to promote the prosperity of one, or more, by sacrificing that of others; and thus to force them to unite in such measures only as would promote the prosperity of all, as the only means to prevent the suspension of the action of the government;—and, thereby, to avoid anarchy, the greatest of all evils. It is by means of such authorized and effectual resistance, that oppression is prevented, and the necessity of resorting to force superseded, in governments of the concurrent majority;—and, hence, compromise, instead of force, becomes their conservative principle.

It would, perhaps, be more strictly correct to trace the conservative principle of constitutional governments to the necessity which compels the different interests, or portions, or orders, to compromise,—as the only way to promote their respective prosperity, and to avoid anarchy,—rather than to the compromise itself. No necessity can be more urgent and imperious, than that of avoiding anarchy. It is the same as that which makes government indispensable to preserve society; and is not less imperative than that which compels obedience to superior force. Traced to this source, the voice of a people,—uttered under the necessity of avoiding the greatest of calamities, through the organs of a government so constructed as to suppress the expression of all partial and selfish interests, and to give a full and faithful utterance to the sense of the whole community, in reference to its common welfare,—may, without impiety, be called *the voice of God.* To call any other so, would be impious.

In stating that force is the conservative principle of absolute, and compromise of constitutional governments, I have assumed both to be perfect in their kind; but not without bearing in mind, that few or none, in fact, have ever been so absolute as not to be under some restraint, and none so perfectly organized as to represent fully and perfectly the voice of the whole community. Such being the case, all must, in practice, depart more or less from the principles by which they are respectively upheld and preserved; and depend more or less for support, on force, or compromise, as the absolute or the constitutional form predominates in their respective organizations.

Nor, in stating that absolute governments exclude all other means of resistance to its authority than that of force, have I overlooked the case of governments of the numerical majority, which form, apparently, an exception. It is true that, in such governments, the minor and subject party, for the time, have the right to oppose and resist the major and dominant party, for the time, through the ballot-box; and may turn them out, and take their place, if they can obtain a majority of votes. But, it is no less true, that this would be a mere change in the relations of the two parties. The minor and subject party would become the major and dominant party, with the same absolute authority and tendency to abuse power; and the major and dominant party would become the minor and subject party, with the same right to resist through the ballot-box; and, if successful, again to change relations, with like effect. But such a state of things must necessarily be temporary. The conflict between the two parties must be transferred, sooner or later, from an appeal to the ballot-box to an appeal to force;—as I shall next proceed to explain.

The conflict between the two parties, in the government of the numerical majority, tends necessarily to settle down into a struggle for the honors and emoluments of the government; and each, in order to obtain an object so ardently desired, will, in the process of the struggle, resort to whatever measure may seem best calculated to effect this purpose. The adoption, by the one, of any measure, however objectionable, which might give it an advantage, would compel the other to follow its example. In such case, it would be indispensable to success to avoid division and keep united;—and hence, from a necessity inherent in the nature of such governments, each party must be alternately forced, in order to insure victory, to resort to measures to concentrate the control over its movements in fewer and fewer hands, as the struggle became more and more violent. This, in process of time, must lead to party organization, and party caucuses and discipline; and these, to the conversion of the honors and emoluments of the government into means of rewarding partisan services, in order to secure the fidelity and increase the zeal of the members of the party. The effect of the whole combined, even in the earlier stages of the process, when they exert the least pernicious influence, would be to place the control of the two parties in the hands of their respective majorities; and the government itself, virtually, under the control of the majority of the dominant party, for the time, instead of the majority of the whole community;—where the theory of this form of government vests it. Thus, in the very first stage of the process, the government becomes the government of a minority instead of a majority;—a minority, usually, and under the most favorable circumstances, of not much more than one-fourth of the whole community.

But the process, as regards the concentration of power, would not stop at this stage. The government would gradually pass from the hands of the majority of the party into those of its leaders; as the struggle became more intense, and the honors and emoluments of the government the all-absorbing objects. At this stage, principles and policy would lose all influence in the elections; and cunning, falsehood, deception, slander, fraud, and gross appeals to the appetites of the lowest and most worthless portions of the community, would take the place of sound reason and wise debate. After these have thoroughly debased and corrupted the community, and all the arts and devices of party have been exhausted, the government would vibrate between the two factions (for such will parties have become) at each successive election. Neither would be able to retain power beyond some fixed term; for those seeking office and patronage would become too numerous to be rewarded by the offices and patronage at the disposal of the government; and these being the sole objects of pursuit, the disappointed would, at the next succeeding election, throw their weight into the opposite scale, in the hope of better success at the next turn of the wheel. These vibrations would continue until confusion, corruption, disorder, and anarchy, would lead to an appeal to force;—to be followed by a revolution in the form of the government. Such must be the end of the government of the numerical majority; and such, in brief, the process through which it must pass, in the regular course of events, before it can reach it.

This transition would be more or less rapid, according to circumstances. The more numerous the population, the more extensive the country, the more diversified the climate, productions, pursuits and character of the people, the more wealthy, refined, and artificial their condition,—and the greater the amount of revenues and disbursements,—the more unsuited would the community be to such a government, and the more rapid would be the passage.

On the other hand, it might be slow in its progress amongst small communities, during the early stages of their existence, with inconsiderable revenues and disbursements, and a population of simple habits; provided the people are sufficiently intelligent to exercise properly, the right of suffrage, and sufficiently conversant with the rules necessary to govern the deliberations of legislative bodies. It is, perhaps, the only form of popular government suited to a people, while they remain in such a condition. Any other would be not only too complex and cumbersome, but unnecessary to guard against oppression, where the motive to use power for that purpose would be so feeble. And hence, colonies, from countries having constitutional governments, if left to themselves, usually adopt governments based on the numerical majority. But as population increases, wealth accumulates, and, above all, the revenues and expenditures become large,—governments of this form must become less and less suited to the condition of society; until, if not in the mean time changed into governments of the concurrent majority, they must end in an appeal to force, to be followed by a radical change in its structure and character; and, most probably, into monarchy in its absolute form,—as will be next explained.

Such, indeed, is the repugnance between popular governments and force,—or, to be more specific,—military power,—that the almost necessary consequence of a resort to force, by such governments, in order to maintain their authority, is, not only a change of their form, but a change into the most opposite,

—that of absolute monarchy. The two are the opposites of each other. From the nature of popular governments, the control of its powers is vested in the many; while military power, to be efficient, must be vested in a single individual. When, then, the two parties, in governments of the numerical majority, resort to force, in their struggle for supremacy, he who commands the successful party will have the control of the government itself. And, hence, in such contests, the party which may prevail, will usually find, in the commander of its forces, a master, under whom the great body of the community will be glad to find protection against the incessant agitation and violent struggles of two corrupt factions, —looking only to power as the means of securing to themselves the honors and emoluments of the government.

From the same cause, there is a like tendency in aristocratical to terminate in absolute governments of the monarchical form; but by no means as strong, because there is less repugnance between military power and aristocratical, than between it and democratical governments.

A broader position may, indeed, be taken; viz., that there is a tendency, in constitutional governments of every form, to degenerate into their respective absolute forms; and, in all absolute governments, into that of the monarchical form. But the tendency is much stronger in constitutional governments of the democratic form to degenerate into their respective absolute forms, than in either of the others; because, among other reasons, the distinction between the constitutional and absolute forms of aristocratical and monarchical governments, is far more strongly marked than in democratic governments. The effect of this is, to make the different orders or classes in an aristocracy, or monarchy, far more jealous and watchful of encroachment on their respective rights; and more resolute and persevering in resisting attempts to concentrate power in any one class or order. On the contrary, the line between the two forms, in popular governments, is so imperfectly understood, that honest and sincere friends of the constitutional form not unfrequently, instead of jealously watching and arresting their tendency to degenerate into their absolute forms, not only regard it with approbation, but employ all their powers to add to its strength and to increase its impetus, in the vain hope of making the government more perfect and popular. The numerical majority, perhaps, should usually be one of the elements of a constitutional democracy; but to make it the sole element, in order to perfect the constitution and make the government more popular, is one of the greatest and most fatal of political errors.

Among the other advantages which governments of the concurrent have over those of the numerical majority,—and which strongly illustrates their more popular character, is,—that they admit, with safety, a much greater extension of the right of suffrage. It may be safely extended in such governments to universal suffrage: that is,—to every male citizen of mature age, with few ordinary exceptions; but it cannot be so far extended in those of the numerical majority, without placing them ultimately under the control of the more ignorant and dependent portions of the community. For, as the community becomes populous, wealthy, refined, and highly civilized, the difference between the rich and the poor will become more strongly marked; and the number of the ignorant and dependent greater in proportion to the rest of the community. With the increase of this difference, the tendency to conflict between them will become stronger; and, as the poor and dependent become more numerous in proportion, there will be, in governments of the numerical majority, no want of leaders among the wealthy and ambitious, to excite and direct them in their efforts to obtain the control.

The case is different in governments of the concurrent majority. There, mere numbers have not the absolute control; and the wealthy and intelligent being identified in interest with the poor and ignorant of their respective portions or interests of the community, become their leaders and protectors. And hence, as the latter would have neither hope nor inducement to rally the former in order to obtain the control, the right of suffrage, under such a government, may be safely enlarged to the extent stated, without incurring the hazard to which such enlargement would expose governments of the numerical majority.

In another particular, governments of the concurrent majority have greatly the advantage. I allude to the difference in their respective tendency, in reference to dividing or uniting the community. That of the concurrent, as has been shown, is to unite the community, let its interests be ever so diversified or opposed; while that of the numerical is to divide it into two conflicting portions, let its interests be, naturally, ever so united and identified.

That the numerical majority will divide the community, let it be ever so homogeneous, into two great parties, which will be engaged in perpetual struggles to obtain the control of the government, has already been established. The great importance of the object at stake, must necessarily form strong party attachments and party antipathies;—attachments on the part of the members of each to their respective parties, through whose efforts they hope to accomplish an object dear to all; and antipathies to the opposite party, as presenting the only obstacle to success.

In order to have a just conception of their force, it must be taken into consideration, that the object to be won or lost appeals to the strongest passions of the human heart,—avarice, ambition, and rivalry. It is not then wonderful, that a form of government, which periodically stakes all its honors and emoluments, as prizes to be contended for, should divide the community into two great hostile parties; or that party attachments, in the progress of the strife, should become so strong among the members of each respectively, as to absorb almost every feeling of our nature, both social and individual; or that their mutual antipathies should be carried to such an excess as to destroy, almost entirely, all sympathy between them, and to substitute in its place the strongest aversion. Nor is it surprising, that under their joint influence, the community should cease to be the common centre of attachment, or that each party should find that centre only in itself. It is thus, that, in such governments, devotion to party becomes stronger than devotion to country ;—the promotion of the interests of party more important than the promotion of the common good of the whole, and its triumph and ascendency, objects of far greater solicitude, than the safety and prosperity of the community. It is thus, also, that the numerical majority, by regarding the community as a unit, and having, as such, the same interests throughout all its parts, must, by its necessary operation, divide it into two hostile parts, waging, under the forms of law, incessant hostilities against each other.

The concurrent majority, on the other hand, tends to unite the most opposite and conflicting interests, and to blend the whole in one common attachment to the country. By giving to each interest, or portion, the power of self-protection, all strife and struggle between them for ascendency, is prevented; and, thereby, not only every feeling calculated to weaken the attachment to the whole is suppressed, but the individual and the social feelings are made to unite in one common devotion to country. Each sees and feels that it can best promote its own prosperity by conciliating the good-will, and promoting the prosperity of the others.

And hence, there will be diffused throughout the whole community kind feelings between its different portions; and, instead of antipathy, a rivalry amongst them to promote the interests of each other, as far as this can be done consistently with the interest of all. Under the combined influence of these causes, the interests of each would be merged in the common interests of the whole; and thus, the community would become a unit, by becoming the common centre of attachment of all its parts. And hence, instead of faction, strife, and struggle for party ascendency, there would be patriotism, nationality, harmony, and a struggle only for supremacy in promoting the common good of the whole.

But the difference in their operation, in this respect, would not end here. Its effects would be as great in a moral, as I have attempted to show they would be in a political point of view. Indeed, public and private morals are so nearly allied, that it would be difficult for it to be otherwise. That which corrupts and debases the community, politically, must also corrupt and debase it morally. The same cause, which, in governments of the numerical majority, gives to party attachments and antipathies such force, as to place party triumph and ascendency above the safety and prosperity of the community, will just as certainly give them sufficient force to overpower all regard for truth, justice, sincerity, and moral obligations of every description. It is, accordingly, found that, in the violent strifes between parties for the high and glittering prize of governmental honors and emoluments,—falsehood, injustice, fraud, artifice, slander, and breach of faith, are freely resorted to, as legitimate weapons;—followed by all their corrupting and debasing influences.

In the government of the concurrent majority, on the contrary, the same cause which prevents such strife, as the means of obtaining power, and which makes it the interest of each portion to conciliate and promote the interests of the others, would exert a powerful influence towards purifying and elevating the character of the government and the people, morally, as well as politically. The means of acquiring power,—or, more correctly, influence,—in such governments, would be the reverse. Instead of the vices, by which it is acquired in that of the numerical majority, the opposite virtues—truth, justice, integrity, fidelity, and all others, by which respect and confidence are inspired, would be the most certain and effectual means of acquiring it.

Nor would the good effects resulting thence be confined to those who take an active part in political affairs. They would extend to the whole community. For of all the causes which contribute to form the character of a people, those by which power, influence, and standing in the government are most certainly and readily obtained, are, by far, the most powerful. These are the objects most eagerly sought of all others by the talented and aspiring; and the possession of which commands the greatest respect and admiration. But, just in proportion to this respect and admiration will be their appreciation by those, whose energy, intellect, and position in society, are calculated to exert the greatest influence in forming the character of a people. If knowledge, wisdom, patriotism, and virtue, be the most certain means of acquiring them, they will be most highly appreciated and assiduously cultivated; and this would cause them to become prominent traits in the character of the people. But if, on the contrary, cunning, fraud, treachery, and party devotion be the most certain, they will be the most highly prized, and become marked features in their character. So powerful, indeed, is the operation of the concurrent majority, in this respect, that, if it were possible for a corrupt and degenerate community to establish and maintain a well-organized government of the kind, it would of itself purify and regenerate them; while, on the other hand, a government based wholly on the numerical majority, would just as certainly corrupt and debase the most patriotic and virtuous people. So great is their difference in this respect, that, just as the one or the other element predominates in the construction of any government, in the same proportion will the character of the government and the people rise or sink in the scale of patriotism and virtue. Neither religion nor education can counteract the strong tendency of the numerical majority to corrupt and debase the people.

If the two be compared, in reference to the ends for which government is ordained, the superiority of the government of the concurrent majority will not be less striking. These, as has been stated, are twofold; to protect, and to perfect society. But to preserve society, it is necessary to guard the community against injustice, violence, and anarchy within, and against attacks from without. If it fail in either, it would fail in the primary end of government, and would not deserve the name.

To perfect society, it is necessary to develope the faculties, intellectual and moral, with which man is endowed. But the main spring to their development, and, through this, to progress, improvement and civilization, with all their blessings, is the desire of individuals to better their condition. For, this purpose, liberty and security are indispensable. Liberty leaves each free to pursue the course he may deem best to promote his interest and happiness, as far as it may be compatible with the primary end for which government is ordained;—while security gives assurance to each, that he shall not be deprived of the fruits of his exertions to better his condition. These combined, give to this desire the strongest impulse of which it is susceptible. For, to extend liberty beyond the limits assigned, would be to weaken the government and to render it incompetent to fulfil its primary end,—the protection of society against dangers, internal and external. The effect of this would be, insecurity; and, of insecurity,—to weaken the impulse of individuals to better their condition, and thereby retard progress and improvement. On the other hand, to extend the powers of the government, so as to contract the sphere assigned to liberty, would have the same effect, by disabling individuals in their efforts to better their condition.

Herein is to be found the principle which assigns to power and liberty their proper spheres, and reconciles each to the other under all circumstances. For, if power be necessary to secure to liberty the fruits of its exertions, liberty, in turn, repays power with interest, by increased population, wealth, and other advantages, which progress and improvement bestow on the community. By thus assigning to each its appropriate sphere, all conflicts between them cease; and each is made to co-operate with and assist the other, in fulfilling the great ends for which government is ordained.

But the principle, applied to different communities, will assign to them different limits. It will assign a larger sphere to power and a more contracted one to liberty, or the reverse, according to circumstances. To the former, there must ever be allotted, under all circumstances, a sphere sufficiently large to protect the community against danger from without and violence and anarchy within. The residuum belongs to liberty. More cannot be safely or rightly allotted to it.

But some communities require a far greater amount of power than others to protect them against anarchy and external dangers; and, of course, the sphere of liberty in such, must be proportionally contracted. The causes calculated to enlarge the one and contract the other, are numerous and various. Some are physical;—such as open and exposed frontiers, surrounded by powerful and hostile neighbors. Others are moral;—such as the different degrees of intelligence, patriotism, and virtue among the mass of the community, and their experience and proficiency in the art of self-government. Of these, the moral are, by far, the most influential. A community may possess all the necessary moral qualifications, in so high a degree, as to be capable of self-government under the most adverse circumstances; while, on the other hand, another may be so sunk in ignorance and vice, as to be incapable of forming a conception of liberty, or of living, even when most favored by circumstances, under any other than an absolute and despotic government.

The principle, in all communities, according to these numerous and various causes, assigns to power and liberty their proper spheres. To allow to liberty, in any case, a sphere of action more extended than this assigns, would lead to anarchy; and this, probably, in the end, to a contraction instead of an enlargement of its sphere. Liberty, then, when forced on a people unfit for it, would, instead of a blessing, be a curse; as it would, in its reaction, lead directly to anarchy,—the greatest of all curses. No people, indeed, can long enjoy more liberty than that to which their situation and advanced intelligence and morals fairly entitle them. If more than this be allowed, they must soon fall into confusion and disorder,—to be followed, if not by anarchy and despotism, by a change to a form of government more simple and absolute; and, therefore, better suited to their condition. And hence, although it may be true, that a people may not have as much liberty as they are fairly entitled to, and are capable of enjoying,—yet the reverse is unquestionably true,—that no people can long possess more than they are fairly entitled to.

Liberty, indeed, though among the greatest of blessings, is not so great as that of protection; inasmuch, as the end of the former is the progress and improvement of the race,—while that of the latter is its preservation and perpetuation. And hence, when the two come into conflict, liberty must, and ever ought, to yield to protection; as the existence of the race is of greater moment than its improvement.

It follows, from what has been stated, that it is a great and dangerous error to suppose that all people are equally entitled to liberty. It is a reward to be earned, not a blessing to be gratuitously lavished on all alike;—a reward reserved for the intelligent, the patriotic, the virtuous and deserving; —and not a boon to be bestowed on a people too ignorant, degraded and vicious, to be capable either of appreciating or of enjoying it. Nor is it any disparagement to liberty, that such is, and ought to be the case. On the contrary, its greatest praise,— its proudest distinction is, that an all-wise Providence has reserved it, as the noblest and highest reward for the development of our faculties, moral and intellectual. A reward more appropriate than liberty could not be conferred on the deserving;— nor a punishment inflicted on the undeserving more just, than to be subject to lawless and despotic rule. This dispensation seems to be the result of some fixed law;—and every effort to disturb or defeat it, by attempting to elevate a people in the scale of liberty, above the point to which they are entitled to rise, must ever prove abortive, and end in disappointment. The progress of a people rising from a lower to a higher point in the scale of liberty, is necessarily slow ;—and by attempting to precipitate, we either retard, or permanently defeat it.

There is another error, not less great and dangerous, usually associated with the one which has just been considered. I refer to the opinion, that liberty and equality are so intimately united, that liberty cannot be perfect without perfect equality.

That they are united to a certain extent,—and that equality of citizens, in the eyes of the law, is essential to liberty in a popular government, is conceded. But to go further, and make equality of *condition* essential to liberty, would be to destroy both liberty and progress. The reason is, that inequality of condition, while it is a necessary consequence of liberty, is, at the same time, indispensable to progress. In order to understand why this is so, it is necessary to bear in mind, that the main spring to progress is, the desire of individuals to better their condition; and that the strongest impulse which can be given to it is, to leave individuals free to exert themselves in the manner they may deem best for that purpose, as far at least as it can be done consistently with the ends for which government is ordained,—and to secure to all the fruits of their exertions. Now, as individuals differ greatly from each other, in intelligence, sagacity, energy, perseverance, skill, habits of industry and economy, physical power, position and opportunity,—the necessary effect of leaving all free to exert themselves to better their condition, must be a corresponding inequality between those who may possess these qualities and advantages in a high degree, and those who may be deficient in them. The only means by which this result can be prevented are, either to impose such restrictions on the exertions of those who may possess them in a high degree, as will place them on a level with those who do not; or to deprive them of the fruits of their exertions. But to impose such restrictions on them would be destructive of liberty,—while, to deprive them of the fruits of their exertions, would be to destroy the desire of bettering their condition. It is, indeed, this inequality of condition between the front and rear ranks, in the march of progress, which gives so strong an impulse to the former to maintain their position, and to the latter to press forward into their files. This gives to progress its greatest impulse. To force the front rank back to the rear, or attempt to push forward the rear into line with the front, by the interposition of the government, would put an end to the impulse, and effectually arrest the march of progress.

These great and dangerous errors have their origin in the prevalent opinion that all men are born free and equal;—than which nothing can be more unfounded and false. It rests upon the assumption of a fact, which is contrary to universal observation, in whatever light it may be regarded. It is, indeed, difficult to explain how an opinion so destitute of all sound reason, ever could have been so extensively entertained, unless we regard it as being confounded with another, which has some semblance of truth;—but which, when properly understood, is not less false and dangerous. I refer to the assertion, that all men are equal in the state of nature; meaning, by a state of nature, a state of individuality, supposed to have existed prior to the social and political state; and in which men lived apart and independent of each other. If such a state ever did exist, all men would have been, indeed, free and equal in it; that is, free to do as they pleased, and exempt from the authority or control of others—as, by supposition, it existed anterior to society and government. But such a state is purely hypothetical. It never did, nor can exist; as it is inconsistent with the preservation and perpetuation of the race. It is, therefore, a great misnomer to call it *the state of nature*. Instead of being the natural state of man, it is, of all conceivable states, the most opposed to his nature—most repugnant to his feelings, and most incompatible with his wants. His natural state is, the social and political—the one for which his Creator made him, and the only one in which he can preserve and perfect his race. As, then, there never was such a state as the, so called, state of nature, and never can be, it follows, that men, instead of being born in it, are born in the social and political state; and of course, instead of being born free and equal, are born subject, not only to parental authority, but to the laws and institutions of the country where born, and under whose protection they draw their first breath. With these remarks, I return from this digression, to resume the thread of the discourse.

It follows, from all that has been said, that the more perfectly a government combines power and liberty,—that is, the greater its power and the more enlarged and secure the liberty of individuals, the more perfectly it fulfils the ends for which government is ordained. To show, then, that the government of the concurrent majority is better calculated to fulfil them than that of the numerical, it is only necessary to explain why the former is better suited to combine a higher degree of power and a wider scope of liberty than the latter. I shall begin with the former.

The concurrent majority, then, is better suited to enlarge and secure the bounds of liberty, because it is better suited to prevent government from passing beyond its proper limits, and to restrict it to its primary end,—the protection of the community. But in doing this, it leaves, necessarily, all beyond it open and free to individual exertions; and thus enlarges and secures the sphere of liberty to the greatest extent which the condition of the community will admit, as has been explained. The tendency of government to pass beyond its proper limits is what exposes liberty to danger, and renders it insecure; and it is the strong counteraction of governments of the concurrent majority to this tendency which makes them so favorable to liberty. On the contrary, those of the numerical, instead of opposing and counteracting this tendency, add to it

increased strength, in consequence of the violent
party struggles incident to them, as has been fully
explained.   And hence their encroachments on liberty, and the danger to which it is exposed under
such governments.

So great, indeed, is the difference between the
two in this respect, that liberty is little more than
a name under all governments of the absolute form,
including that of the numerical majority; and can
only have a secure and durable existence under those
of the concurrent or constitutional form.   The latter, by giving to each portion of the community
which may be unequally affected by its action, a
negative on the others, prevents all partial or local
legislation, and restricts its action to such measures
as are designed for the protection and the good of
the whole.   In doing this, it secures, at the same
time, the rights and liberty of the people, regarded
individually; as each portion consists of those who,
whatever may be the diversity of interests among
themselves, have the same interest in reference to
the action of the government.

Such being the case, the interest of each individual may be safely confided to the majority, or
voice of his portion, against that of all others, and,
of course, the government itself.   It is only through
an organism which vests each with a negative, in
some one form or another, that those who have like
interests in preventing the government from passing
beyond its proper sphere, and encroaching on the
rights and liberty of individuals, can co-operate
peaceably and effectually in resisting the encroach-

ments of power, and thereby preserve their rights and liberty. Individual resistance is too feeble, and the difficulty of concert and co-operation too great, unaided by such an organism, to oppose, successfully, the organized power of government, with all the means of the community at its disposal; especially in populous countries of great extent, where concert and co-operation are almost impossible. Even when the oppression of the government comes to be too great to be borne, and force is resorted to in order to overthrow it, the result is rarely ever followed by the establishment of liberty. The force sufficient to overthrow an oppressive government is usually sufficient to establish one equally, or more, oppressive in its place. And hence, in no governments, except those that rest on the principle of the concurrent or constitutional majority, can the people guard their liberty against power; and hence, also, when lost, the great difficulty and uncertainty of regaining it by force.

It may be further affirmed, that, being more favorable to the enlargement and security of liberty, governments of the concurrent, must necessarily be more favorable to progress, development, improvement, and civilization,—and, of course, to the increase of power which results from, and depends on these, than those of the numerical majority. That it is liberty which gives to them their greatest impulse, has already been shown; and it now remains to show, that these, in turn, contribute greatly to the increase of power.

In the earlier stages of society, numbers and in-

dividual prowess constituted the principal elements
of power. In a more advanced stage, when communities had passed from the barbarous to the civilized
state, discipline, strategy, weapons of increased
power, and money,—as the means of meeting increased expense,—became additional and important
elements. In this stage, the effects of progress and
improvement on the increase of power, began to be
disclosed ; but still numbers and personal prowess
were sufficient, for a long period, to enable barbarous
nations to contend successfully with the civilized,—
and, in the end, to overpower them,—as the pages of
history abundantly testify. But a more advanced
progress, with its numerous inventions and improvements, has furnished new and far more powerful
and destructive implements of offence and defence,
and greatly increased the intelligence and wealth,
necessary to engage the skill and meet the increased
expense required for their construction and application to purposes of war. The discovery of gunpowder, and the use of steam as an impelling force, and
their application to military purposes, have for ever
settled the question of ascendency between civilized
and barbarous communities, in favor of the former.
Indeed, these, with other improvements, belonging
to the present state of progress, have given to communities the most advanced, a superiority over those
the least so, almost as great as that of the latter
over the brute creation. And among the civilized,
the same causes have decided the question of superiority, where other circumstances are nearly equal,
in favor of those whose governments have given the

greatest impulse to development, progress, and improvement; that is, to those whose liberty is the largest and best secured. Among these, England and the United States afford striking examples, not only of the effects of liberty in increasing power, but of the more perfect adaptation of governments founded on the principle of the concurrent, or constitutional majority, to enlarge and secure liberty. They are both governments of this description, as will be shown hereafter.

But in estimating the power of a community, moral, as well as physical causes, must be taken into the calculation; and in estimating the effects of liberty on power, it must not be overlooked, that it is, in itself, an important agent in augmenting the force of moral, as well as of physical power. It bestows on a people elevation, self-reliance, energy, and enthusiasm; and these combined, give to physical power a vastly augmented and almost irresistible impetus.

These, however, are not the only elements of moral power. There are others, and among them harmony, unanimity, devotion to country, and a disposition to elevate to places of trust and power, those who are distinguished for wisdom and experience. These, when the occasion requires it, will, without compulsion, and from their very nature, unite and put forth the entire force of the community in the most efficient manner, without hazard to its institutions or its liberty.

All these causes combined, give to a community its maximum of power. Either of them, without

the other, would leave it comparatively feeble.
But it cannot be necessary, after what has been
stated, to enter into any further explanation or
argument in order to establish the superiority of
governments of the concurrent majority over the
numerical, in developing the great elements of
moral power. So vast is this superiority, that the
one, by its operation, necessarily leads to their development, while the other as necessarily prevents
it,—as has been fully shown.

Such are the many and striking advantages
of the concurrent over the numerical majority.
Against the former but two objections can be made.
The one is, that it is difficult of construction, which
has already been sufficiently noticed; and the other,
that it would be impracticable to obtain the concurrence of conflicting interests, where they were
numerous and diversified; or, if not, that the process for this purpose, would be too tardy to meet,
with sufficient promptness, the many and dangerous
emergencies, to which all communities are exposed.
This objection is plausible; and deserves a fuller
notice than it has yet received.

The diversity of opinion is usually so great, on almost all questions of policy, that it is not surprising,
on a slight view of the subject, it should be thought
impracticable to bring the various conflicting interests of a community to unite on any one line of
policy;—or, that a government, founded on such
a principle, would be too slow in its movements
and too weak in its foundation to succeed in practice. But, plausible as it may seem at the first

glance, a more deliberate view will show, that this opinion is erroneous. It is true, that, when there is no urgent necessity, it is difficult to bring those who differ, to agree on any one line of action. Each will naturally insist on taking the course he may think best;—and, from pride of opinion, will be unwilling to yield to others. But the case is different when there is an urgent necessity to unite on some common course of action; as reason and experience both prove. When something *must* be done,—and when it can be done only by the united consent of all,—the necessity of the case will force to a compromise;—be the cause of that necessity what it may. On all questions of acting, necessity, where it exists, is the overruling motive; and where, in such cases, compromise among the parties is an indispensable condition to acting, it exerts an overruling influence in predisposing them to acquiesce in some one opinion or course of action. Experience furnishes many examples in confirmation of this important truth. Among these, the trial by jury is the most familiar, and on that account, will be selected for illustration.

In these, twelve individuals, selected without discrimination, must unanimously concur in opinion,—under the obligations of an oath to find a true verdict, according to law and evidence; and this, too, not unfrequently under such great difficulty and doubt, that the ablest and most experienced judges and advocates differ in opinion, after careful examination. And yet, as impracticable as this mode of trial would seem to a superficial observer, it is found, in practice, not only to succeed, but to be the safest, the wisest and the best that human ingenuity has ever devised. When closely investigated, the cause will be found in the necessity, under which the jury is placed, to agree unanimously, in order to find a verdict. This necessity acts as the predisposing cause of concurrence in some common opinion; and with such efficacy, that a jury rarely fails to find a verdict.

Under its potent influence, the jurors take their seats with the disposition to give a fair and impartial hearing to the arguments on both sides,—meet together in the jury-room,—not as disputants, but calmly to hear the opinions of each other, and to compare and weigh the arguments on which they are founded;—and, finally, to adopt that which, on the whole, is thought to be true. Under the influence of this *disposition to harmonize*, one after another falls into the same opinion, until unanimity is obtained. Hence its practicability;—and hence, also, its peculiar excellence. Nothing, indeed, can be more favorable to the success of truth and justice, than this predisposing influence caused by the necessity of being unanimous. It is so much so, as to compensate for the defect of legal knowledge, and a high degree of intelligence on the part of those who usually compose juries. If the necessity of unanimity were dispensed with, and the finding of a jury made to depend on a bare majority, jury-trial, instead of being one of the greatest improvements in the judicial department of government, would be one of the greatest evils that could be inflicted on the community. It would be, in such case, the conduit through which all the factious feelings of the day would enter and contaminate justice at its source.

But the same cause would act with still greater force in predisposing the various interests of the community to agree in a well organized government, founded on the concurrent majority. The necessity for unanimity, in order to keep the government in motion, would be far more urgent, and would act under circumstances still more favorable to secure it. It would be superfluous, after what has been stated, to add other reasons in order to show that no necessity, physical or moral, can be more imperious than that of government. It is so much so that, to suspend its action altogether, even for an inconsiderable period, would subject the community to convulsions and anarchy. But in governments of the concurrent majority such fatal consequences can only be avoided by the unanimous concurrence or acquiescence of the various portions of the community. Such is the imperious character of the necessity which impels to compromise under governments of this description.

But to have a just conception of the overpowering influence it would exert, the circumstances under which it would act must be taken into consideration. These will be found, on comparison, much more favorable than those under which juries act. In the latter case there is nothing besides the necessity of unanimity in finding a verdict, and the inconvenience to which they might be subjected in the event of division, to induce juries to agree, except the love of truth and justice, which, when not counteracted by some improper motive or bias, more or less influences all, not excepting the most depraved. In the case of governments of the concurrent majority, there is, besides these, the love of country, than which, if not counteracted by the unequal and oppressive action of government, or other causes, few motives exert a greater sway. It comprehends, indeed, within itself, a large portion both of our individual and social feelings; and, hence, its almost boundless control when left free to act. But the government of the concurrent majority leaves it free, by preventing abuse and oppression, and, with them, the whole train of feelings and passions which lead to discord and conflict between different portions of the community. Impelled by the imperious necessity of preventing the suspension of the action of government, with the fatal consequences to which it would lead, and by the strong additional impulse derived from an ardent love of country, each portion would regard the sacrifice it might have to make by yielding its peculiar interest to secure the common interest and safety of all, including its own, as nothing compared to the evils that would be inflicted on all, including its own, by pertinaciously adhering to a different line of action. So powerful, indeed, would be the motives for concurring, and, under such circumstances, so weak would be those opposed to it, the wonder would be, not that there should, but that there should not be a compromise.

But to form a juster estimate of the full force of this impulse to compromise, there must be added that, in governments of the concurrent majority, each portion, in order to advance its own peculiar interests, would have to conciliate all others, by showing a disposition to advance theirs; and, for this purpose, each would select those to represent it, whose wisdom, patriotism, and weight of character, would command the confidence of the others. Under its influence,—and with representatives so well qualified to accomplish the object for which they were selected,—the prevailing desire would be, to promote the common interests of the whole; and, hence, the competition would be, not which should yield the least to promote the common good, but which should yield the most. It is thus, that concession would cease to be considered a sacrifice,—would become a free-will offering on the altar of the country, and lose the name of compromise. And herein is to be found the feature, which distinguishes governments of the concurrent majority so strikingly from those of the numerical. In the latter, each faction, in the struggle to obtain the control of the government, elevates to power the designing, the artful, and unscrupulous, who, in their devotion to party,—instead of aiming at the good of the whole,—aim exclusively at securing the ascendency of party.

When traced to its source, this difference will be found to originate in the fact, that, in governments of the concurrent majority, individual feelings are, from its organism, necessarily enlisted on the side of the social, and made to unite with them in promoting the interests of the whole, as the best way of promoting the separate interests of each; while, in those of the numerical majority, the social are necessarily enlisted on the side of the individual, and made to contribute to the interest of parties, regardless of that of the whole. To effect the former,—to enlist the individual on the side of the social feelings to promote the good of the whole, is the greatest possible achievement of the science of government; while, to enlist the social on the side of the individual to promote the interest of parties at the expense of the good of the whole, is the greatest blunder which ignorance can possibly commit.

To this, also, may be referred the greater solidity of foundation on which governments of the concurrent majority repose. Both, ultimately, rest on necessity; for force, by which those of the numerical majority are upheld, is only acquiesced in from necessity ; a necessity not more imperious, however, than that which compels the different portions, in governments of the concurrent majority, to acquiesce in compromise. There is, however, a great difference in the motive, the feeling, the aim, which characterize the act in the two cases. In the one, it is done with that reluctance and hostility ever incident to enforced submission to what is regarded as injustice. and oppression; accompanied by the desire and purpose to seize on the first favorable opportunity for resistance:—but in the other, willingly and cheerfully, under the impulse of an exalted patriotism, impelling all to acquiesce in whatever the common good requires.

It is, then, a great error to suppose that the government of the concurrent majority is impracticable;—or that it rests on a feeble foundation. History furnishes many examples of such governments;—and among them, one, in which the principle was carried to an extreme that would be thought impracticable, had it never existed. I refer to that of Poland. In this it was carried to such an extreme that, in the election of her kings, the concurrence or acquiescence of every individual of the nobles and gentry present, in an assembly numbering usually from one hundred and fifty to two hundred thousand, was required to make a choice ; thus giving to each individual a veto on his election. So, likewise, every member of her Diet, (the supreme legislative body,) consisting of the king, the senate, bishops and deputies of the nobility and gentry of the palatinates, possessed a veto on all its proceedings ;—thus making an unanimous vote necessary to enact a law, or to adopt any measure whatever. And, as if to carry the principle to the utmost extent, the veto of a single member not only defeated the particular bill or measure in question, but prevented all others, passed during the session, from taking effect. Further, the principle could not be carried. It, in fact, made every individual of the nobility and gentry, a distinct element in the organism ;—or, to vary the expression, made him an *Estate of the kingdom.* And yet this government lasted, in this form, more than two centuries ; embracing the period of Poland's greatest power and renown. Twice, during its existence, she protected

Christendom, when in great danger, by defeating the Turks under the walls of Vienna, and permanently arresting thereby the tide of their conquests westward.

It is true her government was finally subverted, and the people subjugated, in consequence of the extreme to which the principle was carried; not, however, because of its tendency to dissolution *from weakness*, but from the facility it afforded to powerful and unscrupulous neighbors to control, by their intrigues, the election of her kings. But the fact, that a government, in which the principle was carried to the utmost extreme, not only existed, but existed for so long a period, in great power and splendor, is proof conclusive both of its practicability and its compatibility with the power and permanency of government.

Another example, not so striking indeed, but yet deserving notice, is furnished by the government of a portion of the aborigines of our own country. I refer to the Confederacy of the Six Nations, who inhabited what now is called the western portion of the State of New-York. One chief delegate, chosen by each nation,—associated with six others of his own selection,—and making, in all, forty-two members,—constituted their federal, or general government. When met, they formed the council of the union,—and discussed and decided all questions relating to the common welfare. As in the Polish Diet, each member possessed a veto on its decision; so that nothing could be done without the united consent of all. But this, instead of making the Confederacy weak, or impracticable, had the opposite effect. It secured harmony in council and action, and with them a great increase of power. The Six Nations, in consequence, became the most powerful of all the Indian tribes within the limits of our country. They carried their conquest and authority far beyond the country they originally occupied.

I pass by, for the present, the most distinguished of all these examples;—the Roman Republic;—where the veto, or negative power, was carried, not indeed to the same extreme as in the Polish government, but very far, and with great increase of power and stability;—as I shall show more at large hereafter.

It may be thought,—and doubtless many have supposed, that the defects inherent in the government of the numerical majority may be remedied by a free press, as the organ of public opinion,—especially in the more advanced stage of society,—so as to supersede the necessity of the concurrent majority to counteract its tendency to oppression and abuse of power. It is not my aim to detract from the importance of the press, nor to underestimate the great power and influence which it has given to public opinion. On the contrary, I admit these are so great, as to entitle it to be considered a new and important political element. Its influence is, at the present day, on the increase; and it is highly probable that it may, in combination with the causes which have contributed to raise it to its present importance, effect, in time, great changes,—social and political. But, however important its present influence may be, or may hereafter become,—or, however great and beneficial the changes to which it may ultimately lead, it can never counteract the tendency of the numerical majority to the abuse of power,—nor supersede the necessity of the concurrent, as an essential element in the formation of constitutional governments. These it cannot effect for two reasons, either of which is conclusive.

The one is, that it cannot change that principle of our nature, which makes constitutions necessary to prevent government from abusing its powers,—and government necessary to protect and perfect society.

Constituting, as this principle does, an essential part of our nature,—no increase of knowledge and intelligence, no enlargement of our sympathetic feelings, no influence of education, or modification of the condition of society can change it. But so long as it shall continue to be an essential part of our nature, so long will government be necessary; and so long as this continues to be necessary, so long will constitutions, also, be necessary to counteract its tendency to the abuse of power,—and so long must the concurrent majority remain an essential element in the formation of constitutions. The press may do much,—by giving impulse to the progress of knowledge and intelligence, to aid the cause of education, and to bring about salutary changes in the condition of society. These, in turn, may do much to explode political errors,—to teach how governments should be constructed in order to fulfil their ends; and by what means they can be best preserved, when so constructed. They may, also, do much to enlarge the social, and to restrain the individual feelings;—and thereby to bring about a state of things, when far less power will be required by governments to guard against internal disorder and violence, and external danger; and when, of course, the sphere of power may be greatly contracted and that of liberty proportionally enlarged. But all this would not change the nature of man; nor supersede the necessity of government. For so long as government exists, the possession of its control, as the means of directing its action and dispensing its honors and emoluments, will be an object of desire. While this continues to be the case, it must, in governments of the numerical majority, lead to party struggles; and, as has been shown, to all the consequences, which necessarily follow in their train, and, against which, the only remedy is the concurrent majority.

The other reason is to be found in the nature of the influence, which the press politically exercises.

It is similar, in most respects, to that of suffrage. They are, indeed, both organs of public opinion. The principal difference is, that the one has much more agency in forming public opinion, while the other gives a more authentic and authoritative expression to it. Regarded in either light, the press cannot, of itself, guard any more against the abuse of power, than suffrage; and for the same reason.

If what is called public opinion were always the opinion of the whole community, the press would, as its organ, be an effective guard against the abuse of power, and supersede the necessity of the concurrent majority; just as the right of suffrage would do, where the community, in reference to the action of government, had but one interest. But such is not the case. On the contrary, what is called public opinion, instead of being the united opinion of the whole community, is, usually, nothing more than the opinion or voice of the strongest interest, or combination of interests; and, not unfrequently, of a small, but energetic and active portion of the whole. Public opinion, in relation to government and its policy, is as much divided and diversified, as are the interests of the community; and the press, instead of being the organ of the whole, is usually but the organ of these various and diversified interests respectively; or, rather, of the parties growing out of them. It is used by them as the means of controlling public opinion, and of so moulding it, as to promote their peculiar interests, and to aid in carrying on the warfare of party. But as the organ and instrument of parties, in governments of the numerical majority, it is as incompetent as suffrage itself, to counteract the tendency to oppression and abuse of power;—and can, no more than that, supersede the necessity of the concurrent majority. On the contrary, as the instrument of party warfare, it contributes greatly to increase party excitement, and the violence and virulence of party struggles; and, in the same degree, the tendency to oppression and abuse of power. Instead, then, of superseding the necessity of the

concurrent majority, it increases it, by increasing
the violence and force of party feelings,—in like
manner as party caucuses and party machinery; of
the latter of which, indeed, it forms an important
part.

In one respect, and only one, the government
of the numerical majority has the advantage over
that of the concurrent, if, indeed, it can be called
an advantage. I refer to its simplicity and facility
of construction. It is simple indeed, wielded, as it
is, by a single power—the will of the greater number—and very easy of construction. For this purpose, nothing more is necessary than universal suffrage, and the regulation of the manner of voting,
so as to give to the greater number the supreme control over every department of government.

But, whatever advantages simplicity and facility
of construction may give it, the other forms of absolute government possess them in a still higher
degree. The construction of the government of the
numerical majority, simple as it is, requires some
preliminary measures and arrangements; while the
others, especially the monarchical, will, in its absence,
or where it proves incompetent, force themselves on
the community. And hence, among other reasons,
the tendency of all governments is, from the more
complex and difficult of construction, to the more simple and easily constructed; and, finally, to absolute
monarchy, as the most simple of all. Complexity
and difficulty of construction, as far as they form
objections, apply, not only to governments of the
concurrent majority of the popular form, but to

constitutional governments of every form. The least complex, and the most easily constructed of them, are much more complex and difficult of construction than any one of the absolute forms. Indeed, so great has been this difficulty, that their construction has been the result, not so much of wisdom and patriotism, as of favorable combinations of circumstances. They have, for the most part, grown out of the struggles between conflicting interests, which, from some fortunate turn, have ended in a compromise, by which both parties have been admitted, in some one way or another, to have a separate and distinct voice in the government. Where this has not been the case, they have been the product of fortunate circumstances, acting in conjunction with some pressing danger, which forced their adoption, as the only means by which it could be avoided. It would seem that it has exceeded human sagacity deliberately to plan and construct constitutional governments, with a full knowledge of the principles on which they were formed; or to reduce them to practice without the pressure of some immediate and urgent necessity. Nor is it surprising that such should be the case; for it would seem almost impossible for any man, or body of men, to be so profoundly and thoroughly acquainted with the people of any community which has made any considerable progress in civilization and wealth, with all the diversified interests ever accompanying them, as to be able to organize constitutional governments suited to their condition. But, even were this possible, it would be difficult to find any community sufficiently enlightened and patriotic to adopt such a government, without the compulsion of some pressing necessity. A constitution, to succeed, must spring from the bosom of the community, and be adapted to the intelligence and character of the people, and all the multifarious relations, internal and external, which distinguish one people from another. If it do not, it will prove, in practice, to be, not a constitution, but a cumbrous and useless machine, which must be speedily superseded and laid aside, for some other more simple, and better suited to their condition.

It would thus seem almost necessary that governments should commence in some one of the simple and absolute forms, which, however well suited to the community in its earlier stages, must, in its progress, lead to oppression and abuse of power, and, finally, to an appeal to force,—to be succeeded by a military despotism,—unless the conflicts to which it leads should be fortunately adjusted by a compromise, which will give to the respective parties a participation in the control of the government; and thereby lay the foundation of a constitutional government, to be afterwards matured and perfected. Such governments have been, emphatically, the product of circumstances. And hence, the difficulty of one people imitating the government of another. And hence, also, the importance of terminating all civil conflicts by a compromise, which shall prevent either party from obtaining complete control, and thus subjecting the other.

Of the different forms of constitutional governments, the popular is the most complex and difficult of construction. It is, indeed, so difficult, that ours, it is believed, may with truth be said to be the only one of a purely popular character, of any considerable importance, that ever existed. The cause is to be found in the fact, that, in the other two forms, society is arranged in artificial orders or classes. Where these exist, the line of distinction between them is so strongly marked as to throw into shade, or, otherwise, to absorb all interests which are foreign to them respectively. Hence, in an aristocracy, all interests are, politically, reduced to two,—the nobles and the people; and in a monarchy, with a nobility, into three,—the monarch, the nobles, and the people. In either case, they are so few that the sense of each may be taken separately, through its appropriate organ, so as to give to each a concurrent voice, and a negative on the other, through the usual departments of the government, without making it too complex, or too tardy in its movements to perform, with promptness and energy, all the necessary functions of government.

The case is different in constitutional governments of the popular form. In consequence of the absence of these artificial distinctions, the various natural interests, resulting from diversity of pursuits, condition, situation and character of different portions of the people,—and from the action of the government itself,—rise into prominence, and struggle to obtain the ascendency. They will, it is true, in governments of the numerical majority, ultimately coalesce, and form two great parties; but not so

closely as to lose entirely their separate character
and existence. These they will ever be ready to
re-assume, when the objects for which they coalesced
are accomplished. To overcome the difficulties occasioned by so great a diversity of interests, an organism far more complex is necessary.

Another obstacle, difficult to be overcome, opposes
the formation of popular constitutional governments.
It is much more difficult to terminate the struggles
between conflicting interests, by compromise, in absolute popular governments, than in an aristocracy
or monarchy.

In an aristocracy, the object of the people, in
the ordinary struggle between them and the nobles,
is not, at least in its early stages, to overthrow the
nobility and revolutionize the government,—but to
participate in its powers. Notwithstanding the oppression to which they may be subjected, under
this form of government, the people commonly feel
no small degree of respect for the descendants of a
long line of distinguished ancestors; and do not
usually aspire to more,—in opposing the authority
of the nobles,—than to obtain such a participation
in the powers of the government, as will enable
them to correct its abuses and to lighten their burdens. Among the nobility, on the other hand, it
sometimes happens that there are individuals of
great influence with both sides, who have the good
sense and patriotism to interpose, in order to effect
a compromise by yielding to the reasonable demands
of the people; and, thereby, to avoid the hazard of
a final and decisive appeal to force. It is thus, by a

judicious and timely compromise, the people, in such governments, may be raised to a participation in the administration sufficient for their protection, without the loss of authority on the part of the nobles.

In the case of a monarchy, the process is somewhat different. Where it is a military despotism, the people rarely have the spirit or intelligence to attempt resistance; or, if otherwise, their resistance must almost necessarily terminate in defeat, or in a mere change of dynasty,—by the elevation of their leader to the throne. It is different, where the monarch is surrounded by an hereditary nobility. In a struggle between him and them, both (but especially the monarch) are usually disposed to court the people, in order to enlist them on their respective sides,—a state of things highly favorable to their elevation. In this case, the struggle, if it should be long continued without decisive results, would almost necessarily raise them to political importance, and to a participation in the powers of the government.

The case is different in an absolute Democracy. Party conflicts between the majority and minority, in such governments, can hardly ever terminate in compromise.—The object of the opposing minority is to expel the majority from power; and of the majority to maintain their hold upon it. It is, on both sides, a struggle for the whole,—a struggle that must determine which shall be the governing, and which the subject party;—and, in character, object and result, not unlike that between competitors for the sceptre in absolute monarchies. Its

regular course, as has been shown, is, excessive violence,—an appeal to force,—followed by revolution,—and terminating at last, in the elevation to supreme power of the general of the successful party.
And hence, among other reasons, aristocracies and
monarchies more readily assume the constitutional
form than absolute popular goverments.

Of the three different forms, the monarchical has
heretofore been much the most prevalent, and, gen-
erally, the most powerful and durable. This result
is doubtless to be attributed principally to the fact
that, in its absolute form, it is the most simple and
easily constructed. And hence, as government is
indispensable, communities having too little intelligence to form or preserve the others, naturally fall
into this. It may also, in part, be attributed to
another cause, already alluded to; that, in its organism and character, it is much more closely assimilat-
ed than either of the other two, to military power;
on which all absolute governments depend for support. And hence, also, the tendency of the others,
and of constitutional governments which have been
so badly constructed or become so disorganized as
to require force to support them,—to pass into military despotism,—that is, into monarchy in its most
absolute and simple form. And hence, again, the
fact, that revolutions in absolute monarchies, end, almost invariably, in a change of dynasty,—and not of
the forms of the government; as is almost univer-
sally the case in the other systems.

But there are, besides these, other causes of a
higher character, which contribute much to make

monarchies the most prevalent, and, usually, the most durable governments. Among them, the leading one is, they are the most susceptible of improvement;—that is, they can be more easily and readily modified, so as to prevent, to a limited extent, oppression and abuse of power, without assuming the constitutional form, in its strict sense. It slides, almost naturally, into one of the most important modifications. I refer to hereditary descent. When this becomes well defined and firmly established, the community or kingdom, comes to be regarded by the sovereign as the hereditary possession of his family,—a circumstance which tends strongly to identify his interests with those of his subjects, and thereby, to mitigate the rigor of the government. It gives, besides, great additional security to his person; and prevents, in the same degree, not only the suspicion and hostile feelings incident to insecurity,—but invites all those kindly feelings which naturally spring up on both sides, between those whose interests are identified,—when there is nothing to prevent it. And hence the strong feelings of paternity on the side of the sovereign,—and of loyalty on that of his subjects, which are often exhibited in such governments.

There is another improvement of which it is readily susceptible, nearly allied to the preceding. The hereditary principle not unfrequently extends to other families,—especially to those of the distinguished chieftains, by whose aid the monarchy was established, when it originates in conquest. When this is the case,—and a powerful body of hereditary nobles surround the sovereign, they oppose a strong resistance to his authority, and he to theirs,—tending to the advantage and security of the people. Even when they do not succeed in obtaining a participation in the powers of the government, they usually acquire sufficient weight to be felt and respected. From this state of things, such governments usually, in time, settle down on some fixed rules of action, which the sovereign is compelled to respect, and by which increased protection and security are acquired by all. It was thus the enlightened monarchies of Europe were formed, under which the people of that portion of the globe have made such great advances in power, intelligence, and civilization.

To these may be added the greater capacity, which governments of the monarchical form have exhibited, to hold under subjection a large extent of territory, and a numerous population; and which has made them more powerful than others of a different form, to the extent, that these constitute an element of power. All these causes combined, have given such great and decisive advantages, as to enable them, heretofore, to absorb, in the progress of events, the few governments which have, from time to time, assumed different forms;—not excepting even the mighty Roman Republic, which, after attaining the highest point of power, passed, seemingly under the operation of irresistible causes, into a military despotism. I say, heretofore,—for it remains to be seen whether they will continue to retain their advantages, in these respects, over the others, under the great and growing influence of public opinion, and the new and imposing form which popular government has assumed with us.

These have already effected great changes, and will probably effect still greater,—adverse to the monarchical form ; but, as yet, these changes have tended rather to the absolute, than to the constitutional form of popular government,—for reasons which have been explained. If this tendency should continue permanently in the same direction, the monarchical form must still retain its advantages, and continue to be the most prevalent. Should this be the case, the alternative will be between monarchy and popular government, in the form of the numerical majority,—or absolute democracy; which, as has been shown, is not only the most fugitive of all the forms, but has the strongest tendency of all others to the monarchical. If, on the contrary, this tendency, or the changes referred to, should incline to the constitutional form of popular government,—and a proper organism come to be regarded as not less indispensable than the right of suffrage to the establishment of such governments,—in such case, it is not improbable that, in the progress of events, the monarchical will cease to be the prevalent form of government. Whether they will take this direction, at least for a long time, will depend on the success of our government,—and a correct understanding of the principles on which it is constructed.

To comprehend more fully the force and bearing of public opinion, and to form a just estimate of the changes to which, aided by the press, it will probably lead, politically and socially,—it will be necessary to consider it in connection with the causes that have given it an influence so great, as to entitle it to be regarded as a new political element. They will, upon investigation, be found in the many discoveries and inventions made in the last few centuries.

Among the more prominent of those of an earlier date, stand the practical application of the magnetic power to the purposes of navigation, by the invention of the mariner's compass; the discovery of the mode of making gunpowder, and its application to the art of war ; and the invention of the art of printing. Among the more recent are, the numerous chemical and mechanical discoveries and inventions, and their application to the various arts of production ; the application of steam to machinery of almost every description, especially to such as is designed to facilitate transportation and travel by land and water ; and, finally, the invention of the magnetic telegraph.

All these have led to important results. Through the invention of the mariner's compass, the globe has been circumnavigated and explored, and all who inhabit it, with but few exceptions, brought within the sphere of an all-pervading commerce, which is daily diffusing over its surface the light and blessings of civilization. Through that of the art of printing, the fruits of observation and reflection, of discoveries and inventions, with all the accumulated stores of previously acquired knowledge, are preserved and widely diffused. The application of gunpowder to the art of war, has for ever settled the long conflict for ascendency between civilization and barbarism, in favor of the former, and thereby guarantied that, whatever knowledge is now accumulated, or may hereafter be added, shall never again be lost. The numerous discoveries and inventions, chemical and mechanical, and the application of steam to machinery, have increased, many-fold, the productive powers of labor and capital; and have, thereby, greatly increased the number, who may devote themselves to study and improvement, —and the amount of means necessary for commercial exchanges,—especially between the more and the less advanced and civilized portions of the globe, —to the great advantage of both, but particularly of the latter. The application of steam to the purposes of travel and transportation, by land and water, has vastly increased the facility, cheapness and rapidity of both;—diffusing, with them, information and intelligence almost as quickly and as freely as if borne by the winds; while the electrical wires outstrip them, in velocity—rivalling, in rapidity, even thought itself.

The joint effect of all has been, a great increase and diffusion of knowledge; and, with this, an impulse to progress and civilization heretofore unexampled in the history of the world,—accompanied by a mental energy and activity unprecedented.

To all these causes, public opinion, and its organ, the press, owe their origin and great influence. Already they have attained a force in the more civilized portions of the globe sufficient to be felt by all governments, even the most absolute and despotic. But, as great as they now are, they have as yet attained nothing like their maximum force. It is probable, that not one of the causes, which have contributed to their formation and influence, has yet produced its full effect; while several of the most powerful have just begun to operate; and many others, probably of equal or even greater force, yet remain to be brought to light.

When the causes now in operation have produced their full effect, and inventions and discoveries shall have been exhausted,—if that may ever be,—they will give a force to public opinion, and cause changes, political and social, difficult to be anticipated. What will be their final bearing, time only can decide with any certainty. That they will, however, greatly improve the condition of man ultimately,—it would be impious to doubt. It would be to suppose, that the all-wise and beneficent Being,—the Creator of all,—had so constituted man, as that the employment of the high intellectual faculties, with which He has been pleased to endow him, in order that he might develop the laws that control the great agents of the material world, and make them subservient to his use,—would prove to him the cause of permanent evil,—and not of permanent good. If, then, such a supposition be inadmissible, they must, in their orderly and full development, end in his permanent good. But this cannot be, unless the ultimate effect of their action, politically, shall be, to give ascendency to that form of government best calculated to fulfil the ends for which government is ordained. For, so completely does the well-being of our race depend on good government, that it is hardly possible any change, the ultimate effect of which should be otherwise, could prove to be a permanent good.

It is, however, not improbable, that many and great, but temporary evils, will follow the changes they have effected, and are destined to effect. It seems to be a law in the political, as well as in the material world, that great changes cannot be made, except very gradually, without convulsions and revolutions; to be followed by calamities, in the beginning, however beneficial they may prove to be in the end. The first effect of such changes, on long established governments, will be, to unsettle the opinions and principles in which they originated,—and which have guided their policy,—before those, which the changes are calculated to form and establish, are fairly developed and understood. The interval between the decay of the old and the formation and establishment of the new, constitutes a period of transition, which must always necessarily be one of uncertainty, confusion, error, and wild and fierce fanaticism.

The governments of the more advanced and civilized portions of the world are now in the midst of this period. It has proved, and will continue to prove a severe trial to existing political institutions of every form. Those governments which have not the sagacity to perceive what is truly public opinion,—to distinguish between it and the mere clamor of faction, or shouts of fanaticism,—and the good sense and firmness to yield, timely and cautiously, to the claims of the one,—and to resist, promptly and decidedly, the demands of the other,—are doomed to fall. Few will be able successfully to pass through this period of transition; and these, not without shocks and modifications, more or less considerable. It will endure until the governing and the governed shall better understand the ends for which government is ordained, and the form best adapted to accomplish them, under all the circumstances in which communities may be respectively placed.

I shall, in conclusion, proceed to exemplify the elementary principles, which have been established, by giving a brief account of the origin and character of the governments of Rome and Great Britain; the two most remarkable and perfect of their respective forms of constitutional governments. The object is to show how these principles were applied, in the more simple forms of such governments; preparatory to an exposition of the mode in which they have been applied in our own more complex system. It will appear that, in each, the principles are the same; and that the difference in their application resulted from the different situation and social condition of the respective communities. They were modified, in each, so as to conform to these; and, hence, their remarkable success. They were applied to communities in which hereditary rank had long prevailed. Their respective constitutions originated in concession to the people; and, through them, they acquired a participation in the powers of government. But with us, they were applied to communities where all political rank and distinction between citizens were excluded; and where government had its origin in the will of the people.

But, however different their origin and character, it will be found that the object in each was the same, —to blend and harmonize the conflicting interests of the community; and the means the same,—taking the sense of each class or portion through its appropriate organ, and considering the concurrent sense of all as the sense of the whole community. Such being the fact, an accurate and clear conception how this was effected, in their more simple forms, will enable us better to understand how it was accomplished in our far more refined, artificial, and complex form.

It is well known to all, the least conversant with their history, that the Roman people consisted of two distinct orders, or classes,—the Patricians and the Plebeians; and that the line of distinction was so strongly drawn, that, for a long time, the right of intermarriage between them was prohibited. After the overthrow of the monarchy and the expulsion of the Tarquins, the government fell exclusively under the control of the patricians, who, with their clients and dependents, formed, at the time, a very numerous and powerful body. At first, while there was danger of the return of the exiled family, they treated the plebeians with kindness; but, after it had passed away, with oppression and cruelty.

It is not necessary, with the object in view, to enter into a minute account of the various acts of oppression and cruelty to which they were subjected. It is sufficient to state, that, according to the usages of war at the time, the territory of a conquered people became the property of the conquerors; and that the plebeians were harassed and oppressed by incessant wars, in which the danger and toil were theirs, while all the fruits of victory, (the lands of the vanquished, and the spoils of war,) accrued to the benefit of their oppressors. The result was such as might be expected. They were impoverished, and forced, from necessity, to borrow from the patricians, at usurious and exorbitant interest, funds with which they had been enriched through their blood and toil; and to pledge their all for repayment at stipulated periods. In case of default, the pledge became forfeited; and, under the provisions of law in such cases, the debtors were liable to be seized, and sold or imprisoned by their creditors in private jails prepared and kept for the purpose. These savage provisions were enforced with the utmost rigor against the indebted and impoverished plebeians. They constituted, indeed, an essential part of the system through which they were plundered and oppressed by the patricians.

A system so oppressive could not be endured. The natural consequences followed. Deep hatred was engendered between the orders, accompanied by factions, violence, and corruption, which distracted and weakened the government. At length, an incident occurred which roused the indignation of the plebeians to the utmost pitch, and which ended in an open rupture between the two orders.

An old soldier, who had long served the country, and had fought with bravery in twenty-eight battles, made his escape from the prison of his creditor, —squalid, pale, and famished. He implored the protection of the plebeians. A crowd surrounded him; and his tale of service to the country, and the cruelty with which he had been treated by his creditor, kindled a flame, which continued to rage until it extended to the army. It refused to continue any longer in service,—crossed the Anio, and took possession of the sacred mount. The patricians divided in opinion as to the course which should be pursued. The more violent insisted on an appeal to arms, but, fortunately, the counsel of the moderate, which recommended concession and compromise, prevailed. Commissioners were appointed to treat with the army; and a formal compact was entered into between the orders, and ratified by the oaths of each, which conceded to the plebeians the right to elect two tribunes, as the protectors of their order, and made their persons sacred. The number was afterwards increased to ten, and their election by centuries changed to election by tribes;—a mode by which the plebeians secured a decided preponderance.

Such was the origin of the tribunate;—which, in process of time, opened all the honors of the government to the plebeians. They acquired the right, not only of vetoing the passage of all laws, but also their execution; and thus obtained, through their tribunes, a negative on the entire action of the government, without divesting the patricians of their control over the Senate. By this arrangement, the government was placed under the concurrent and joint voice of the two orders, expressed through separate and appropriate organs; the one possessing the positive, and the other the negative powers of the government. This simple change converted it from an absolute, into a constitutional government,—from a government of the patricians only, to that of the whole Roman people,—and from an aristocracy into a republic. In doing this, it laid the solid foundation of Roman liberty and greatness.

A superficial observer would pronounce a government, so organized, as that one order should have the power of making and executing the laws, and another, or the representatives of another, the unlimited authority of preventing their enactment and execution,—if not wholly impracticable, at least, too feeble to stand the shocks to which all governments are subject; and would, therefore, predict its speedy dissolution, after a distracted and inglorious career.

How different from the result! Instead of distraction, it proved to be the bond of concord and harmony; instead of weakness, of unequalled strength;—and, instead of a short and inglorious career, one of great length and immortal glory. It moderated the conflicts between the orders; harmonized their interests, and blended them into one; substituted devotion to country in the place of devotion to particular orders; called forth the united strength and energy of the whole, in the hour of danger; raised to power, the wise and patriotic; elevated the Roman name above all

others; extended her authority and dominion over
the greater part of the then known world, and
transmitted the influence of her laws and institutions to the present day. Had the opposite counsel prevailed at this critical juncture; had an appeal
been made to arms instead of to concession and
compromise, Rome, instead of being what she afterwards became, would, in all probability, have been
as inglorious, and as little known to posterity as
the insignificant states which surrounded her, whose
names and existence would have been long since
consigned to oblivion, had they not been preserved
in the history of her conquests of them. But
for the wise course then adopted, it is not improbable,—whichever order might have prevailed,—
that she would have fallen under some cruel and
petty tyrant;—and, finally, been conquered by
some of the neighboring states,—or by the Cartha-
ginians, or the Gauls. To the fortunate turn which
events then took, she owed her unbounded sway
and imperishable renown.

It is true, that the tribunate, after raising her
to a height of power and prosperity never before
equalled, finally became one of the instruments by
which her liberty was overthrown:—but it was not
until she became exposed to new dangers, growing
out of increase of wealth and the great extent of
her dominions, against which the tribunate furnished no guards. Its original object was the protection of the plebeians against oppression and abuse
of power on the part of the patricians. This, it
thoroughly accomplished; but it had no power to

protect the people of the numerous and wealthy conquered countries from being plundered by consuls and proconsuls. Nor could it prevent the plunderers from using the enormous wealth, which they extorted from the impoverished and ruined provinces, to corrupt and debase the people; nor arrest the formation of parties, (irrespective of the old division of patricians and plebeians,) having no other object than to obtain the control of the government for the purpose of plunder. Against these formidable evils, her constitution furnished no adequate security. Under their baneful influence, the possession of the government became the object of the most violent conflicts; not between patricians and plebeians,—but between profligate and corrupt factions. They continued with increasing violence, until, finally, Rome sunk, as must every community under similar circumstances, beneath the strong grasp, the despotic rule of the chieftain of the successful party;—the sad, but only alternative which remained to prevent universal violence, confusion and anarchy. The Republic had, in reality, ceased to exist long before the establishment of the Empire. The interval was filled by the rule of ferocious, corrupt and bloody factions. There was, indeed, a small but patriotic body of eminent individuals, who struggled, in vain, to correct abuses, and to restore the government to its primitive character and purity;—and who sacrificed their lives in their endeavors to accomplish an object so virtuous and noble. But it can be no disparagement to the tribunate, that the great powers conferred on it for wise purposes, and which it had so fully accomplished, should be seized upon, during this violent and corrupt interval, to overthrow the liberty it had established, and so long nourished and supported.

In assigning such consequence to the tribunate, I must not overlook other important provisions of the Constitution of the Roman government. The Senate, as far as we are informed, seems to have been admirably constituted to secure consistency and steadiness of action. The power,—when the Republic was exposed to imminent danger,—to appoint a dictator,—vested, for a limited period, with almost boundless authority; the two consuls, and the manner of electing them; the auguries; the sibylline books; the priesthood, and the censorship;—all of which appertained to the patricians,—were, perhaps indispensable to withstand the vast and apparently irregular power of the tribunate;—while the possession of such great powers by the patricians, made it necessary to give proportionate strength to the only organ through which the plebeians could act on the government with effect. The government was, indeed, powerfully constituted; and, apparently, well proportioned both in its positive and negative organs. It was truly an iron government. Without the tribunate, it proved to be one of the most oppressive and cruel that ever existed; but with it, one of the strongest and best.

The origin and character of the British government are so well known, that a very brief sketch, with the object in view, will suffice.

The causes which ultimately moulded it into its

present form, commenced with the Norman Conquest. This introduced the feudal system, with its necessary appendages, a hereditary monarchy and nobility; the former in the line of the chief, who led the invading army;—and the latter in that of his distinguished followers. They became his feudatories. The country,—both land and people,—(the latter as serfs,) was divided between them. Conflicts soon followed between the monarch and the nobles,—as must ever be the case under such systems. They were followed, in the progress of events, by efforts, on the part both of monarchs and nobles, to conciliate the favor of the people. They, in consequence, gradually rose to power. At every step of their ascent, they became more important,—and were more and more courted,—until at length their influence was so sensibly felt, that they were summoned to attend the meeting of parliament by delegates; not, however, as an estate of the realm, or constituent member of the body politic. The first summons came from the nobles; and was designed to conciliate their good feelings and secure their co-operation in the war against the king. This was followed by one from him; but his object was simply to have them present at the meeting of parliament, in order to be *consulted* by the crown, on questions relating to taxes and supplies; not, indeed, to discuss the right to lay the one, and to raise the other,—for the King claimed the arbitrary authority to do both,—but with a view to facilitate their collection, and to reconcile them to their imposition.

From this humble beginning, they, after a long

struggle, accompanied by many vicissitudes, raised themselves to be considered one of the estates of the realm; and, finally, in their efforts to enlarge and secure what they had gained, overpowered, for a time, the other two estates; and thus concentrated all power in a single estate or body. This, in effect, made the government absolute, and led to consequences which, as by a fixed law, must ever result in popular governments of this form;—namely:— to organized parties, or, rather, factions, contending violently to obtain or retain the control of the government; and this, again, by laws almost as uniform, to the concentration of all the powers of government in the hands of the military commander of the successful party.

His heir was too feeble to hold the sceptre he had grasped; and the general discontent with the result of the revolution, led to the restoration of the old dynasty; without defining the limits between the powers of the respective estates.

After a short interval, another revolution followed, in which the lords and commons united against the king. This terminated in his overthrow; and the transfer of the crown to a collateral branch of the family, accompanied by a declaration of rights, which defined the powers of the several estates of the realm; and, finally, perfected and established the constitution. Thus, a feudal monarchy was converted, through a slow but steady process of many centuries, into a highly refined constitutional monarchy, without changing the basis of the original government.

As it now stands, the realm consists of three estates; the king; the lords temporal and spiritual; and the commons. The parliament is the grand council. It possesses the supreme power. It enacts laws, by the concurring assent of the lords and commons,—subject to the approval of the king. The executive power is vested in the monarch, who is regarded as constituting the first estate. Although irresponsible himself, he can only act through responsible ministers and agents. They are responsible to the other estates; to the lords, as constituting the high court before whom all the servants of the crown may be tried for malpractices, and crimes against the realm, or official delinquencies;—and to the commons, as possessing the impeaching power, and constituting the grand inquest of the kingdom. These provisions, with their legislative powers,— especially that of withholding supplies,—give them a controlling influence on the executive department, and, virtually, a participation in its powers;—so that the acts of the government, throughout its entire range, may be fairly considered as the result of the concurrent and joint action of the three estates;— and, as these embrace all the orders,—of the concurrent and joint action of the estates of the realm.

He would take an imperfect and false view of the subject who should consider the king, in his mere individual character, or even as the head of the royal family,—as constituting an estate. Regarded in either light, so far from deserving to be considered as the First Estate,—and the head of the realm, as he is,—he would represent an interest too inconsiderable to be an object of special protection. Instead of this, he represents what in reality is, habitually and naturally, the most powerful interest, all things considered, under every form of government in all civilized communities,—*the tax-consuming interest;* or, more broadly, the great interest which necessarily grows out of the action of the government, be its form what it may;—the interest that *lives by the government.* It is composed of the recipients of its honors and emoluments; and may be properly called, the government interest, or party;—in contradistinction to the rest of the community,—or, (as they may be properly called,) the people or commons. The one comprehends all who are supported by the government;—and the other all who support the government:—and it is only because the former are strongest, all things being considered, that they are enabled to retain, for any considerable time, advantages so great and commanding.

This great and predominant interest is naturally represented by a single head. For it is impossible, without being so represented, to distribute the honors and emoluments of the government among those who compose it, without producing discord and conflict:—and it is only by preventing these, that advantages so tempting can be long retained. And, hence, the strong tendency of this great interest to the monarchical form;—that is, to be represented by a single individual. On the contrary, the antagonistic interest,—that which supports the government, has the opposite tendency;— a tendency to be represented by many; because a large assembly can better judge, than one individual or a few, what burdens the community can bear;—and how it can be most equally distributed, and easily collected.

In the British government, the king constitutes an Estate, because he is the head and representative of this great interest. He is the conduit through which, all the honors and emoluments of the government flow;—while the House of Commons, according to the theory of the government, is the head and representative of the opposite—the great tax-paying interest, by which the government is supported.

Between these great interests, there is necessarily a constant and strong tendency to conflict; which, if not counteracted, must end in violence and an appeal to force,—to be followed by revolution, as has been explained. To prevent this, the House of Lords, as one of the estates of the realm, is interposed; and constitutes the conservative power of the government. It consists, in fact, of that portion of the community who are the principal recipients of the honors, emoluments, and other advantages derived from the government; and whose condition cannot be improved, but must be made worse by the triumph of either of the conflicting estates over the other; and, hence, it is opposed to the ascendency of either,—and in favor of preserving the equilibrium between them.

This sketch, brief as it is, is sufficient to show, that these two constitutional governments,—by far the most illustrious of their respective kinds,—conform to the principles that have been established, alike in their origin and in their construction. The constitutions of both originated in a pressure, occasioned by conflicts of interests between hostile classes or orders, and were intended to meet the pressing exigencies of the occasion; neither party, it would seem, having any conception of the principles involved, or the consequences to follow, beyond the immediate objects in contemplation. It would, indeed, seem almost impossible for constitutional governments, founded on orders or classes, to originate in any other manner. It is difficult to conceive that any people, among whom they did not exist, would, or could voluntarily institute them, in order to establish such governments; while it is not at all wonderful, that they should grow out of conflicts between different orders or classes when aided by a favorable combination of circumstances.

The constitutions of both rest on the same principle;—an organism by which the voice of each order or class is taken through its appropriate organ; and which requires the concurring voice of all to constitute that of the whole community. The effects, too, were the same in both;—to unite and harmonize conflicting interests;—to strengthen attachments to the whole community, and to moderate that to the respective orders or classes; to rally all, in the hour of danger, around the standard of their country; to elevate the feeling of nationality, and to develop power, moral and physical, to an extraordinary extent. Yet each has its distinguishing features, resulting from the difference of their organisms, and the circumstances in which they respectively originated.

In the government of Great Britain, the three orders are blended in the legislative department; so that the separate and concurring act of each is necessary to make laws; while, on the contrary, in the Roman, one order had the power of making laws, and another of annulling them, or arresting their execution. Each had its peculiar advantages. The Roman developed more fully the love of country and the feelings of nationality. "*I am a Roman citizen*,"—was pronounced with a pride and elevation of sentiment, never, perhaps, felt before or since, by any citizen or subject of any community, in announcing the country to which he belonged.

It also developed more fully the power of the community. Taking into consideration their respective population, and the state of the arts at the different periods, Rome developed more power, comparatively, than Great Britain ever has,—vast as that is, and has been,—or, perhaps, than any other community ever did. Hence, the mighty control she acquired from a beginning so humble. But the British government is far superior to that of Rome, in its adaptation and capacity to embrace under its control extensive dominions, without subverting its constitution. In this respect, the Roman constitution was defective;—and, in consequence, soon began to exhibit marks of decay, after Rome had extended her dominions beyond Italy; while the British holds under its sway, without apparently impairing either, an empire equal to that, under the weight of which the constitution and liberty of Rome were crushed. This great advantage it derives from its different

structure, especially that of the executive department; and the character of its conservative principle. The former is so constructed as to prevent, in
consequence of its unity and hereditary character,
the violent and factious struggles to obtain the control of the government,—and, with it, the vast patronage which distracted, corrupted, and finally subverted the Roman Republic. Against this fatal
disease, the latter had no security whatever; while
the British government,—besides the advantages it
possesses, in this respect, from the structure of its
executive department,—has, in the character of its
conservative principle, another and powerful security against it. Its character is such, that patronage,
instead of weakening, strengthens it:—For, the greater the patronage of the government, the greater
will be the share which falls to the estate constituting the conservative department of the government; and the more eligible its condition, the greater
its opposition to any radical change in its form.
The two causes combined, give to the government a
greater capacity of holding under subjection extensive dominions, without subverting the constitution
or destroying liberty, than has ever been possessed
by any other. It is difficult, indeed, to assign any
limit to its capacity in this respect. The most probable which can be assigned is, its ability to bear
increased burdens;—the taxation necessary to meet
the expenses incident to the acquisition and government of such vast dominions, may prove, in the end,
so heavy as to crush, under its weight, the laboring
and productive portions of the population.

I have now finished the brief sketch I proposed, of the origin and character of these two renowned governments; and shall next proceed to consider the character, origin and structure of the Government of the United States. It differs from the Roman and British, more than they differ from each other; and, although an existing government of recent origin, its character and structure are perhaps less understood than those of either.

Printed in the USA
CPSIA information can be obtained
at www.ICGtesting.com
LVHW092147131223
766472LV00005B/58